THE NATIONAL DEPRESSIVE AND MANIC-DEPRESSIVE ASSOCIATION

RESTORING INTIMACY

THE PATIENT'S GUIDE TO MAINTAINING RELATIONSHIPS DURING DEPRESSION

WITH A FOREWORD AND
CONTRIBUTIONS BY
DREW PINSKY, M.D.

ANITA H. CLAYTON, M.D.
DAVID L. DUNNER, M.D.
ROBERT M.A. HIRSCHFELD, M.D.
MARTHA M. MANNING, PH.D.
LAURA EPSTEIN ROSEN, PH.D.
THOMAS N. WISE, M.D.

NATIONAL
DM
DA

RESTORING INTIMACY:
THE PATIENT'S GUIDE TO MAINTAINING
RELATIONSHIPS DURING DEPRESSION

A National Depressive and Manic-Depressive Association
(National DMDA) Book/October 1999

National DMDA would like to acknowledge the contributions of Linda Carbone, book editor, Nancy Field, book designer, and Anthony Russo, cover artist, without whom this book would not have been possible. The organization would also like to thank Paul E. Keck, Jr., M.D. and Mark M. Gottlieb for reviewing the manuscript.

Restoring Intimacy was sponsored by an educational grant from Glaxo Wellcome, Inc.

Certain portions of this book have previously appeared in publications including National DMDA literature and *When Someone You Love Is Depressed* by Laura Epstein Rosen, Ph.D. and Xavier Francisco Amador, Ph.D.

Published and printed in the United States of America

ISBN 0-9673893-0-5

Library of Congress Number: 99-074689

National Depressive and Manic-Depressive Association
730 North Franklin Street, Suite 501
Chicago, IL 60610-3526 USA

BVG 10 9 8 7 6 5 4 3 2 1

One can only gain higher ground by climbing up through the valley.
—PHILLIP KELLER

This book is dedicated to all who have courageously climbed through the valley of depression and to those who journey with them.

CONTENTS

**National DMDA:
Your Resource for Education and Support / vii**

Foreword / xi

CHAPTER 1
Diagnosing Depression / 1

What Is Depression? / 3
Who Is Likely to Be Affected and for How Long? / 9

CHAPTER 2
Treating Depression / 15

Psychotherapy (Talk Therapy) / 17
Medication / 20
Medication Treatment and Side Effects / 28
Depression in Men versus Women / 36

CHAPTER 3
**Relationship Issues:
Dealing with Depression Together / 43**

Helping Yourself or Your Partner Identify
and Get Treated for Depression / 45
Helping Yourself or Your Partner
through Sexual Dysfunction / 50
Dealing with the Strain on Your Emotional Intimacy / 55
When You Both Suffer from Depression / 65
When There Are Children at Home / 67

CHAPTER 4

Getting the Help You Need / 71

Finding the Doctor You Need / 73
Problems with Insurance Coverage / 77

CHAPTER 5

Resources / 81

Self Tests / 83
Where to Go for Additional Information or Help / 93
Recommended Reading / 103
Medications Currently Prescribed to Treat Depression / 104
Contributor Biographies / 107
Index / 111

NATIONAL DMDA:
YOUR RESOURCE FOR
EDUCATION AND SUPPORT

The National Depressive and Manic-Depressive Association (National DMDA) is the largest patient-run, illness-specific organization in the United States. Founded in 1986 and headquartered in Chicago, Illinois, National DMDA has a grassroots network of nearly 300 chapters and support groups. It is guided by a 65-member Scientific Advisory Board composed of the leading researchers and clinicians in the field of depressive illnesses.

National DMDA's mission is to educate patients, families, professionals, and the public concerning the nature of depressive and manic-depressive illnesses as *treatable* medical diseases; to foster self-help for patients and families; to eliminate discrimination and stigma; to improve access to care; and to advocate for research toward the elimination of these illnesses.

Every month, thousands of people call our toll-free information line and log on to our web site. Most people contact National DMDA because they want information about depression or manic-depressive illness (bipolar disorder) or they want a referral to a DMDA support group.

MEETING OUR MISSION

National DMDA works to meet each component of its mission:

PROVIDING EDUCATION

National DMDA reaches out through print, video, and the Internet to provide the latest information on depression and manic depression. Dozens of National DMDA brochures provide easy-to-understand descriptions of the illnesses and discuss the latest treatment options. All publications are available at no cost or for a nominal fee. Our Web site keeps visitors up to date on National DMDA's current events, activities, and research findings. For a listing of available publications, log on to the National DMDA web site (www.ndmda.org) or call our toll-free information line (800-826-3632).

FOSTERING SELF HELP

DMDA support groups help consumers help themselves. Groups are patient-run and participation is free of charge for those with limited incomes. According to a recent survey, DMDA groups motivate people to follow their treatment plans and make follow-up visits to their doctors. The survey also found that those active in support groups were less likely to stop taking medication against medical advice and were more willing to tolerate medication side effects. They also might be less likely to be hospitalized. For a DMDA group in your community, contact National DMDA.

ELIMINATING DISCRIMINATION AND STIGMA

National DMDA is your voice in the fight to recognize depression and manic depression as treatable medical illnesses, not flaws in a person's character. National DMDA responds to media coverage that misrepresents people with depressive disorders. Also, National DMDA's Legal Committee participates in Supreme Court cases concerning issues of importance to people with depressive disorders.

IMPROVING ACCESS TO CARE

National DMDA sounds its voice to protect consumers from unfair insurance practices. We educate the public on how to look for quality in a behavioral health care company. National DMDA reviews government plans for mental health services and responds when the consumer is not protected. National DMDA informs the public of clinical trials and educates participants on ways they can protect themselves. We advocate for insurance parity and unrestricted pharmaceutical formularies.

ADVOCATING FOR RESEARCH

National DMDA submits written statements to the U.S. Congress on the need for enhanced research into the causes of, and better treatments for, depressive disorders, and advocates for increased federal spending for research. We also review the ethics of psychiatric research on human subjects.

JOIN US!

By becoming a member of National DMDA, you show your support of our mission. In addition, members of National DMDA receive a variety of services, including:

- *Support Groups* conducted by local chapters provide a forum for patients and family members to share coping skills and build self-esteem. Many mental health professionals recommend National DMDA groups for people who otherwise may feel alone or victimized by their illness. Being active in a support group gives you the opportunity to reach out to others and to benefit from the experience of those who have "been there." There are nearly 300 patient-run DMDA chapters across the United States.

- A *Bookstore* with more than 70 titles of printed and audiovisual materials focusing on depressive disorders and related topics. All bookstore items are available at a discount for National DMDA members.

- *Outreach,* the official newsletter of National DMDA, is mailed quarterly to members. It covers research and treatment, consumer awareness, advocacy updates and delivers a strong message of hope.

- *Free Information* is mailed to anyone who calls our toll-free number. Contacting National DMDA is often the first step a person takes toward finding help for themselves, a family member, co-worker, or friend.

- *Helpful Staff,* some who have experienced a depressive illness, is available to offer guidance. Although National DMDA does not operate as a crisis hotline or offer medical advice, you will always find someone to direct you to the help you need.

- *Annual Conferences* where leading experts in the field join patients, family members, and members of the advocacy community. Registration fees are reduced for National DMDA members.

- *Education Programs* including Mental Health Month, the Campaign on Clinical Depression, National Depression Screening Day, and a number of education videos. These programs emphasize the importance of recognizing symptoms, getting an early diagnosis, and receiving proper treatment.

- *A Voice in Washington, DC.* National DMDA advocates to improve availability and quality of health care, to eliminate discrimination and stigma, and to increase research toward the elimination of these illnesses.

HOW TO REACH NATIONAL DMDA:

National Depressive and Manic-Depressive Association
730 N. Franklin Street, Suite 501
Chicago, Illinois 60610-3526 USA
Phone: (800) 826-3632 or (312) 642-0049
Fax: (312) 642-7243
www.ndmda.org

National DMDA does not endorse or recommend the use of any specific treatment or medication mentioned in this publication. For advice about specific treatment or medication, patients should consult their physicians and/or mental health professionals.

FOREWORD

By Dr. Drew Pinsky

Depression can shatter the foundation of even the most solid relationship. As partners struggle against the fallout of guilt, confusion, and anger, genuine affection and intimacy often become all but impossible to maintain. Even the most compassionate and insightful partners can find themselves helplessly watching their depressed mates withdraw into islands of despair.

I know the desperation of these individuals because I've talked to many of them over the years in my clinical practice. And I know that their feeling of letting their partners down can be as devastating as the depression itself. This sense of failing their partners occurs in part because of a loss of interest in sex, which is a common symptom of depression as well as a side effect of some antidepressant medications.

Both partners in a relationship troubled by depression have a pressing need for information on how to salvage their emotional and physical connection to one another. The idea of filling this need was the spark that led to the creation of this book. We hope that *Restoring Intimacy: The Patient's Guide to Maintaining Relationships During Depression* provides valuable coping strategies for anyone who is, or whose partner is, clinically depressed. Written in plain English and conceived by the National Depressive and Manic-Depressive Association—the nation's leading organization for information and support for those who suffer from these disorders—it brings together the expertise of seven noted authorities to answer many difficult questions about depression's effect on intimacy.

My esteemed colleagues and I explore the role of talk therapy for both individuals and couples. We discuss some of the medications used to treat depression and their possible side effects. We also provide advice on how to reconnect with your partner and loved ones when the depression is doing everything it can to keep you apart.

We hope that this book will help couples get back on track after depression has derailed their relationship. It can help provide an oasis of love and intimacy as you make your journey through the storm.

CHAPTER 1

DIAGNOSING DEPRESSION

WHAT IS DEPRESSION?

How can I help my loved ones understand that what I'm going through isn't something I can just "snap out of "? And how can I help them understand exactly what is going on inside?

It can be an extra challenge to have this conversation when you have depression. Here are some ideas: make a comparison between depression and other medical illnesses, like diabetes, chronic asthma, or heart disease. People don't tell others with these diseases to "snap out of it," why would they say it to someone with depression? Because we know depression can be as disabling as any of these other illnesses, it is important to seek treatment. And while you can be treated for it, there may occasionally be flare-ups that need more attention.

It is also helpful to ask them to read brochures, self-help books, and memoirs on the topic. You can also get videotapes of people talking about their own experiences with depression from mental health organizations (see the Resource section at the back of this book). When people realize that well-known people like Mike Wallace and Tipper Gore have suffered from depression, it can make a big impression. It can help validate your experience and put it into language they can understand. This can be very comforting for your loved ones. You can also invite them to a session with your therapist or doctor.

—Dr. Martha Manning

The best way to educate yourself and your family is through information from organizations that deal with the illness, like the National Depressive and Manic-Depressive Association (National DMDA), talking with your mental health professional, and seeking out books and pamphlets that help explain this is a medical illness, not a personal weakness. (See the Resource section at the back of this book.)

Of course, you may also be feeling irritable and shut off from your loved ones—not exactly the best time to get yourself to the library or onto the Internet. Ask them to get involved. It will help them to better understand what you are experiencing.

—DR. DAVID DUNNER

Nearly 20 million Americans experience depression each year, and more than 15 percent will die from this illness. But somehow our culture has difficulty coming to terms with what we now know about this medical condition. It is a disorder of brain chemistry in which the brain's mood center functions at a lower-than-usual level. While one's individual experiences and environment contribute to the cause and course of depression, once the biology has been set off balance, it usually can not be resolved by "being strong." Depression is not under the control of your will, or something you can merely "snap out of."

It's important for people to understand what is and what is not a disease. Disease is a complex relationship between the genetic makeup of the individual and the environment in which that individual exists. The interaction of the two creates an abnormality that results in signs and symptoms that progress in a predictable pattern, and which have a predictable response to treatment. Depression fits this definition and is therefore not a character weakness or personality flaw.

We know from research that genetics play a part in the susceptibility to depression, but one's environment also has a strong role in the onset and progression of the disease. We also now know that an imbalance occurs in brain chemistry during depression. It has been measured and recorded by scientists.

—DR. DREW PINSKY

What's the difference between normal grieving or feeling down about things that happen in life, like a marriage failing or losing a job, and clinical depression?

You may feel down because of relationship problems or stressed because you got laid off from your job. You may be overwhelmed by grief because someone you love has died. Grieving is the price we pay for caring about someone. We may feel a sense of longing, which may express itself as waves of anguish or as the feeling that a person we loved is still around. These feelings are normal. They are not signs of clinical depression, although one-third of grieving people may in fact become clinically depressed if the feelings don't subside within a reasonable length of time.

Clinical depression is a constant state, and a real medical illness. It exhibits certain characteristics, such as loss of interest in things you used to enjoy, loss of energy, difficulty concentrating, difficulty sleeping or sleeping too much, drastic changes in eating (too much or too little), lowered sexual drive, and in some cases suicidal thoughts. These signs and symptoms are like an exaggeration of ordinary sadness, and they create a steady mood that does not lift for weeks or much longer. If you experience any of these symptoms for longer than two weeks, you should seek help from a mental health professional or your primary care physician.

—DR. THOMAS WISE

I have heard that there are different types and severity levels of depression. What are they?

The two main ways to distinguish between types of depression are according to (1) whether the depression is a single episode or recurring episodes, and (2) whether or not it is chronic.

Chronic depression is defined as continuing for two years or more. For most chronically depressed patients, the illness has gone on for many years. (Some patients describe a feeling of having been depressed for as long as they can remember.) *Dysthymia* is a chronic mild depression.

Other types of depression include:

Psychotic depression, which involves delusions and hearing voices, even voices that may tell you to kill yourself. Psychotically depressed people are at great risk of suicide.

Manic depression, also called bipolar disorder, alternates periods of depression with periods of highs. During a manic phase you need less sleep, talk more rapidly, have a heightened interest in sex, over-estimate your abilities, and are generally more driven. To some people this sounds pretty good until they realize that a manic phase might drive them to run through all their savings or believe they're the most special or powerful person on earth. It can be terribly embarrassing for you and those around you. You can also be extremely irritable and angry during a manic phase.

All these types of depression can be mild, moderate, or severe, depending on the extent and severity of your symptoms. They require different treatments and an accurate diagnosis is essential.

—DR. ROBERT HIRSCHFELD

SYMPTOMS OF DEPRESSION:

- Persistent sadness
- Feelings of worthlessness
- Excessive guilt
- Difficulty concentrating
- Trouble organizing thoughts
- Difficulty remembering
- Fatigue
- Loss of connection to past interests
- Changes in eating
- Increase or decrease in sleeping
- Loss of interest in sex
- Disconnection
- Persistent physical complaints
- Thoughts of death or suicide

How can I tell whether I'm just exhausted or heading into depression? Is there a way to know? Can I avoid a bout of clinical depression?

If you are heading into a depression, you will experience a group of symptoms that do not lift. Exhaustion may be one of these symptoms, but you could be fatigued because you're overworked or not getting enough sleep or feeling a lot of stress. A combination of depressive symptoms that do not go away for several weeks distinguishes the disorder from conditions such as exhaustion.

As for avoiding a bout with depression, it may sound simplistic, but thinking positively may head it off in some cases. If you feel you have options and close friends to talk to, you may succeed in driving away a mild depression that was about to grip you. Of course, in severe cases, no thought is going to lift you out of the depression that is looming. As soon as you are aware of the warning signs—loss of interest in things you used to enjoy, loss of energy, difficulty concentrating, difficulty sleeping, changes in appetite, lowered sexual drive, and in some cases suicidal thoughts—get treatment. The sooner you get help, the less time you will have to spend suffering.

—Dr. Thomas Wise

Where can I get more information about treatment options for depression? I think I may have depression and I don't know where to begin.

There are many great resources available today to help people learn about and get treatment for depression (see the Resource section at the back of this book). It can take a lot of energy to do research on depression when you are in the midst of it. But there is a common list of symptoms to help you identify whether you have depression: persistent sadness, low mood, sleep and appetite disturbances, loss of energy, cognitive impairment, sometimes suicidal thoughts.

Depression screening days are held in communities across the country every year. You can fill out a confidential form that asks basic questions about symptoms of depression and speak with a professional who will give you feedback and a referral if you need it. You can also call or visit the Web sites of the major mental health organizations, such as National DMDA. (See the Resource section at the back of this book.)

Many people feel comfortable talking to a member of the clergy as a starting point.

—DR. MARTHA MANNING

I was recently diagnosed with depression and two of my symptoms were exhaustion and fatigue. Since I started therapy and began taking medication, I feel better, but the fatigue seems to have gotten worse. Will I ever feel energetic again?

Low energy is often the slowest symptom to respond to treatment. It's not uncommon to continue to feel tired long after your other symptoms have shown improvement. You should wait a few more weeks to see if you begin to feel a difference. Or your doctor might find it necessary to change the dose of your medication and/or add a second medication to help increase your energy level. However, stimulants might cause anxiety, agitation, or insomnia. Always be sure to talk to your doctor about possible side effects of any proposed medication.

—DR. ROBERT HIRSCHFELD

I am 28 years old, and I am feeling extremely sad and crying a lot, and lately I have been very lazy. My doctor told me that this behavior is not abnormal for someone my age. He said most likely the feelings will go away on their own. Can this be right?

All of the symptoms you describe are signs of depression; they can also be symptoms of other medical conditions. Even though I have been chief of medicine in a psychiatric hospital for many years, I am still surprised at how often depression can be hidden by or triggered by other medical conditions.

If these symptoms continue for more than two weeks and your doctor has ruled out other medical conditions, and your symptoms are not related to drug or alcohol abuse, then it's time to be evaluated for depression.

You deserve a complete and thorough medical evaluation based on your symptoms. You should go back to your physician and talk about your concerns. If your physician still insists that there is nothing to worry about, but these symptoms become persistent and disabling, you need to see another doctor for a second opinion. Once other medical problems are ruled out, you may want to consider seeing a psychologist or psychiatrist.

Depression is a potentially fatal illness. It is important to be accurately diagnosed and treated without delay.

—DR. DREW PINSKY

WHO IS LIKELY TO BE AFFECTED AND FOR HOW LONG?

Is there a cure for depression? If not, does that mean I'll have to battle symptoms all my life?

There is no cure for depression, but effective treatments are available. Think about other illnesses for which this is also true: diabetes, arthritis, high blood pressure, thyroid imbalance, and most heart diseases. Depression tends to be a recurrent illness. After each episode, your risk of a recurrence increases.

Yes, there are people for whom the battle against symptoms of depression will be lifelong. Your doctor can help determine whether you are one of them. The good news is that treatment is effective and safe for long-term use.

—DR. ROBERT HIRSCHFELD

WHO GETS DEPRESSION?

- People of all ages, races, ethnic groups, and economic classes
- Those with depression in their family
- Women, twice as often as men

If someone in my immediate family has clinical depression, what are the chances that I will also become depressed?

We know that the predisposition to depression involves multiple genes. In some families, every member has depression. In others, there may be just one person with the illness. But family members are definitely at increased risk, and the more members with depression within a family, the higher the risk.

Women whose immediate family members have been clinically depressed will be twice as likely to fall prey to depression as men. Men with depression in the immediate family are at risk of developing depression and also of abusing alcohol or other drugs.

—Dr. Anita Clayton

Is it possible for people to experience depression for the first time when they are in their sixties or seventies? My parents are in that age range and I am concerned about their well-being.

Yes, it is certainly possible. A first depressive episode usually occurs in your twenties or thirties, but it's not uncommon to have your first one later in life. When that happens, it must be taken very seriously; a first episode in an older person is more likely to be severe and to have psychotic features. The danger of suicide is very real, so you are right to be concerned.

It's important to rule out other possible medical factors that could be responsible for the symptoms (like fatigue or inability to concentrate) your parents may be exhibiting. A problem such as thyroid disturbance or a blood disease could include symptoms of depression. Even the side effects of certain medications, such as those for blood pressure, could include depression. Senility or dementia might also be responsible. Your parents' physician will need to be careful to rule out these other possibilities. If it is indeed depression, psychotherapy and/or antidepressant medication can provide a solution.

One of the reasons depression might not show up until late in life is because it might have been triggered by events like chronic illness, major changes in lifestyle such as retirement, or the loss of a husband or wife—common life events for people in their sixties and seventies. But, as with a person with depression of any age, the illness can be treated. Be sure your parents talk to their doctor. Offer to go with them if you think that will help.

—DR. ROBERT HIRSCHFELD

What percentage of people will relapse or have a recurrence after being successfully treated for depression?

Studies tell us that if you've had one episode, there's a 50 percent likelihood of recurrence after recovery. If you've had three or more episodes, that probability leaps to 90 percent. If you suffer every year, or more than once a year, you may be suffering from seasonal depression or recurrent depression with mild highs—bipolar rather than unipolar disorder. You're considered chronically depressed if you've suffered for two years or more. Partial treatment may be the danger in this case: if a full course of treatment isn't followed, you will tend to relapse.

It's important to know the difference between recurrence and relapse. *Recurrence* means a new episode after a period of recovery. *Relapse* means you haven't fully recovered from an episode of depression and your symptoms have flared up again.

—DR. DAVID DUNNER

TREATING DEPRESSION

- Depression is a very treatable illness—more than 80 percent of people treated respond positively
- Diagnosis from a physician or mental health professional is the first step
- There are many ways to manage the symptoms of depression
- A combination of medication, counseling, support from family and friends, and a local support group is usually the best treatment

I have been undergoing both psychiatric and medication treatment for my depression, but nothing seems to be helping. I have been feeling very down and more alone than ever. Recently, for the first time, I have been thinking of suicide. What should I do?

Depression can make you begin to think about death in the abstract and then about ending your own life. Many people with depression are frightened and ashamed of these thoughts and don't want to admit them to anyone. It's critically important for you to share them with others. Talk to your doctor about it. If you feel you're in immediate danger, find someone to talk to right away and get yourself to an emergency room. *More than 15 percent of people with untreated or undertreated depression take their own lives—seek help immediately if you are thinking of suicide.*

Suicidal thoughts can be very dangerous, especially when those thoughts lose their scariness and become attractive. No matter how frightened or ashamed they make you feel, you must talk about these thoughts with a friend, a family member, or a doctor. Never forget that suicide is a tragic, permanent solution to a temporary problem.

—DR. MARTHA MANNING

IF YOU HAVE THOUGHTS OF SUICIDE

- It's critically important for you to share your thoughts of suicide with someone else. If you feel you're in immediate danger, find someone to talk to right away and get yourself to an emergency room
- Take any thought of suicide seriously. More than 15 percent of people with untreated or undertreated depression take their own lives
- Never forget that suicide is a tragic, permanent solution to a temporary problem
- National suicide hotline: 800-999-9999
- Call 911 or a local crisis line

CHAPTER 2

TREATING DEPRESSION

PSYCHOTHERAPY (TALK THERAPY)

I want to find a therapist, but don't know how, and I don't have any friends who can recommend one. How do I start the process?

There are many different mental health professionals with different areas of expertise, so you may feel overwhelmed at first. But finding help is easier than you might think. Start with your primary care doctor. Other good resources are hospitals, psychology departments of local universities, and medical schools. You can even ask your local librarian for books or for lists of therapists in the area—perhaps saying that you're doing research for a project, in order to maintain your privacy. Organizations such as National DMDA can also be great places to get advice about support groups in your area; group members can share their personal experiences.

To narrow down your search, it's helpful to understand that different professionals have received different kinds of training. A *psychiatrist* has been through medical school and psychiatry residency training, and is the only mental health professional who can prescribe medication. A *psychologist* with a Ph.D. has had six to eight years of doctoral training and an internship in a hospital. A licensed *clinical social worker* has at least two years of postgraduate training and is licensed to practice psychotherapy in a particular state. Additional clinical training hours are required to maintain their license. In general, social workers are particularly helpful with referrals to a variety of social service agencies. *Psychotherapist* is a general term for anyone in the mental health field, and *counselor* is a general term for someone with a bachelor's or associate's degree who is trained to offer therapy. Counselors are usually associated with a clinic.

The most important factor is not which kind of professional you choose, but the type of relationship you feel you can develop with the person. You want to find someone you feel you can trust, someone you can talk to openly about your symptoms and your innermost thoughts. It's a good idea to interview a few possible therapists, then have one or two consultations with the one you pick before making a commitment. Keep in mind that you can always change your mind later if you feel unsatisfied with how the therapy is progressing.

—DR. LAURA EPSTEIN ROSEN

Doesn't every person with depression take antidepressant medication these days? Do I really need the "talking cure" too?

Antidepressant medication is the cornerstone to treating depression. The medical literature is very clear on this. Equally clear, however, is that for complete remission, psychotherapy—on an individual basis, in a group, or for couples—is extremely important.

A qualified physician can properly assess whether antidepressant medication is recommended. It may not be. In some cases, talk therapy may be appropriate. If the depression is recurrent, however, antidepressants (together with therapy) may provide relief from your pain and suffering. In cases where the depression has disabling and potentially dangerous symptoms such as suicidal thoughts, stabilization of mood with medication becomes medically urgent. Once your mood is stabilized and you are out of danger, the more time-consuming process of psychotherapy can then proceed.

—DR. DREW PINSKY

My husband was just diagnosed with clinical depression. He's taking an antidepressant but isn't getting any therapy along with it. How successful will his treatment be?

The good news is that there are many excellent treatment options today for depression. Medication and psychotherapy have been shown to be equally effective, except for severe depression or bipolar illness (manic depression)—for people with these illnesses, antidepressant medications tend to work faster and better. Most professionals today agree that the best way to treat depression is with both medication and therapy.

That doesn't mean that your husband will necessarily have a better result if psychotherapy is added. His antidepressant medication will help improve his mood and other symptoms. However, if he's had a long-term depression that has left him with (for example) self-doubts and relationship problems, talk therapy would certainly be called for so that he can work on these longstanding issues. Therapy is also a benefit to people who want to stop taking medication as soon as their symptoms begin to lift, or who feel a lot of shame about their condition and their need for medication. These important issues should be discussed with a mental health professional before stopping medication. Typically, the symptoms of a recurrence become obvious sooner when a person is in therapy.

Your husband's comfort with these various options is of critical importance. Would he be willing to see a therapist, or is he dead set against it? What does *he* think would be most helpful for him? If he sees his depression only in biological terms, chances are he will be satisfied just taking antidepressant medication. For some people, this takes away the stigma of having an "emotional" problem. If he knows he has other problems that he needs to talk to someone about, he may be open to therapy. You might gently introduce the subject by mentioning you've heard that antidepressants work well if combined with talk therapy. But rest assured that the medication alone should resolve his depressive symptoms.

Another excellent option to consider is attending a National DMDA support group. It has been shown that support groups help people stay on their treatment plan, can help people deal with the shame they feel about having depression, and can provide a valuable network for patients and their families.

—DR. LAURA EPSTEIN ROSEN

What about short-term therapies, like cognitive behavioral ther-apy, for treating depression? How well do they work?

For mild depression, short-term therapies may work about as well as antidepressant medication. For moderate depression, it's less clear, but they can be about as effective as antidepressants. For severe depression, antidepressants work better than therapy. A combination of medication and therapy may be best for some people, especially those who are severely depressed.

Among short-term therapies, interpersonal therapy, which focuses on relationships (your reactions to others and theirs to you), may work best for women. Men tend to respond better to cognitive behavioral therapy, which emphasizes thoughts and behaviors that you may be relying on but that don't work for you. Cognitive behavioral therapy will teach you to interrupt those thoughts and behaviors in order to arrive at different results.

—Dr. Anita Clayton

MEDICATION

After beginning antidepressant medication treatment, how soon before my partner is "back to normal"?

It can be very frustrating when someone finally decides to be treated for depression to learn that it often takes four to six weeks, or even longer, for full restoration of mood. There is great individual variabil-ity: some people respond sooner, and about one-third won't respond at all to the first medication. If you don't respond, your doctor has choices, such as increasing your dosage, supplementing it with another medication, or trying a new medication. With adjustments, 85 to 90 percent of people can expect to see improvements.

You also may see improvement with certain symptoms while oth-ers take longer to subside. For example, sleep difficulties and anxiety may show quicker improvement. The depressed mood itself may take longer. It can be a gradual process, so be patient.

No matter how quickly or how well your symptoms improve, your doctor may recommend you stay on the antidepressant medication for at least a year. Some doctors recommend two to five years. We now know, for example, that many people will likely relapse if they've had three depressive episodes before the age of 40, two before the age of 50, or one after 50. Following your doctor's prescribed plan is the best way to stay safe from depression's grasp again. Otherwise you may notice the same symptoms returning.

—Dr. Thomas Wise

I have been treated for depression with an antidepressant medication for the past six months. How long do I have to stay on it and should I talk to my mental health professional about going off it? I'm afraid of relapse and I've heard that after symptoms go away, people still need to take their medication. Why?

Guidelines for treatment include three phases. In the *acute* phase, your doctor will make sure you are recovered. This takes about eight to 12 weeks. The *continuation* phase goes on for four to six months. On average, depression is approximately a nine-month illness, and the continuation phase ensures this period of time will be covered. The antidepressant medication might be reduced at the end of the continuation phase, especially if it's your first episode. You'd be observed during this phase and for four to six months afterward.

Maintenance treatment can go on for five to seven years after depression has subsided, to protect against recurrence for patients who have had prior episodes. There is some discussion among mental health experts about lifetime maintenance treatment for people with several episodes of recurrent depression, but this is not yet included as part of the official guidelines.

—Dr. David Dunner

If I am experiencing side effects, should I switch medication? I am worried that switching may cause a relapse of my depression.

There are a lot of ways to deal with this, so the first step is to talk to your doctor. He or she may recommend decreasing your dose or adding other antidepressant or anti-anxiety medication to counteract the side effects. If you switch medication, be aware that the new one may cause side effects, too. There is the possibility, as you mention, of relapsing if you switch medications to one that doesn't work for you. But chances are good that you will respond well if one has already worked for you. If, however, you tried several medications before finding one that works, your doctor will no doubt recommend that you stick with that one. As always, honest and open communication with your doctor is key in the treatment of your depression.

—DR. ROBERT HIRSCHFELD

How do I know my antidepressant medication is working? How different will I feel?

You probably won't feel all that different after starting a prescription for an antidepressant. The most common experience my patients describe is that things that used to seem overwhelming "don't bother me so much." There are some objective tools your doctor may use to measure whether or not the antidepressant medication has had a reasonable effect. What you should expect and take notice of is relief from symptoms such as crying, thoughts of suicide, panic or anxiety, and excessive changes in sleep patterns and appetite.

—DR. DREW PINSKY

The goal for you, if you're taking an antidepressant and have had a major depressive episode, should be to return to your baseline level of functioning—the level you were at before you became depressed. People with dysthymia, people who've suffered chronic mild depression, may find after taking antidepressant medications that they feel better than they've ever felt in their lives. They feel freed up from what was holding them back from being who they are. For other types of depression, you will just feel that your symptoms are gone. You'll be yourself again.

It's important to understand that it might take several weeks before the medication has a full effect. It's very important not to miss doses. Also, do not stop taking your antidepressant when you begin feeling better. Your antidepressant is a medication for an illness, and you need to follow your doctor's instructions carefully. Be sure to see your doctor regularly during the early period, in order to review your symptoms and any side effects the medication may be causing.

Usually, physical symptoms will show improvement first. For example, sleep and appetite problems might improve, then you'll notice a return of interest in activities and an increase in your sex drive, then an improved mood. Finally you will have the overall feeling that you're no longer depressed. Although the people close to you will notice the earlier improvements, you might not feel really well until the last stage. But the medication will have been working all along.

—DR. ANITA CLAYTON

I have read that there are more than 20 antidepressant medications. How does the doctor know which medication to try first?

Tricyclics, an older group of antidepressants, would not likely be tried first, since the newer antidepressants, including the selective serotonin reuptake inhibitors (SSRIs), have fewer side effects, are not as dangerous if too high a dose is accidentally taken, and sometimes need to be taken only once a day.

Your doctor's choice of what to try first will be based on a combination of factors, starting with your symptoms. If you are very anxious, for example, your doctor will prescribe a drug that will be less likely to increase your anxiety. If you're excessively fatigued, you'll get something that will help energize you. If you're having a lot of trouble sleeping, the doctor will use a more sedating drug. Your doctor will usually start with a smaller dose, then increase as necessary. Of course, the choice will also be affected by any other medications you are taking that might interact with the new antidepressant.

Some people have more difficulty than others in taking medication more than once a day. An antidepressant that can be taken only once a day may make it easier for them to stay on the medication to achieve its benefit. After six months on antidepressants, only half of patients will still be taking them. If they feel better, if they experience side effects like sexual problems, or if they're worried about the cost, they may simply stop taking their medication. This can be very problematic since we now know that longer-term use offers the best results. It's important to talk to your doctor. Never decide on your own to change your dose or stop taking your medications.

—DR. THOMAS WISE

Most medications work for about the same percentage of people. Approximately 60 to 70 percent of people treated with their first antidepressant will respond to it. Fifty percent of those will return to their level of functioning before the depression hit, and another 20 percent will improve somewhat, but not get back to their baseline state. However, it's hard to predict what will work for a particular individual.

In deciding which antidepressant to prescribe for you, your doctor will try to match up the symptoms of your depression with the potential effects of the medication (both therapeutic effects and side effects). For example, an anxious patient will be given a calming medication.

—DR. ANITA CLAYTON

I'm a college student and two major things happened to me within weeks of each other: I started taking an antidepressant medication and I got my first boyfriend. But I can't reach orgasm when we have sex. Could this be caused by the medication?

First it's important to determine whether the problem started when you began taking the antidepressant medication and whether the difficulty in achieving orgasm has just been with sexual intercourse, or if you had difficulty achieving orgasm under any circumstances, for example by masturbation.

If your situation started with the use of the antidepressant, you should return to the doctor who prescribed the medication and tell him or her what's going on. One of the most common side effects that I hear about from people taking antidepressant medication is difficulty with sexual functioning—and difficulty reaching orgasm is one of the complaints. You should know that there are alternative treatments that are less likely to cause this side effect. Your doctor could switch you to another medication, or add a medication to reverse this side effect.

It's also important to communicate with your partner about your difficulty achieving orgasm and about what gives you pleasure. This communication won't be easy, but it is necessary. When you express your feelings to your partner, no matter how difficult this may be, your partner will be better able to support you, thus positively affecting your ability to recover.

Again, communication with your physician about sexual dysfunction is essential. Don't be embarrassed. There's probably nothing you could say that your doctor hasn't heard before. When it comes to medication, your health care professional is the only one who can provide the answers.

—DR. DREW PINSKY

My boyfriend has started to take antidepressant medication, but is still drinking heavily. Won't drinking just make his depression worse? I'm worried he'll become angry if I try to talk to him about this.

Both alcohol and drug abuse make depression worse. Also, both make it difficult for the antidepressant treatment to work, may interact dangerously with it, or may reduce its effect. Suicide rates are also higher for people with depression who drink alcohol—most suicide attempts take place in depressed patients while under its influence.

Tell your boyfriend that you're concerned and that you would like to go with him to his next doctor visit. With the permission of your boyfriend, the doctor should be happy to meet with the two of you. I personally recommend that people with depression include their partners at doctor visits to talk about treatment planning—that way I'm getting better information from both parties and the person with depression has support from the partner in following the treatment plan. If he gets angry, all you can do is show your support and concern. You may also choose to seek counseling for yourself if the situation results in significant stress for you.

—DR. DAVID DUNNER

People often use drinking as a kind of self-medication when they're feeling depressed. If your boyfriend just started on antidepressant medication, he may still feel depressed and may be drinking to mask those feelings. Alcohol can weaken the effectiveness of some antidepressants. Either way, your boyfriend should deal with his drinking problem. He may think it's making him feel better, but alcohol is a depressant: in the long term, it will make his illness worse.

When you bring it up to him, tell him you're concerned that the drinking might be making his depression worse. Be sure to put your statements in terms of yourself, not him, otherwise it may sound as if you're attacking him. Say "I'm concerned about you. I've noticed that you've been drinking while taking this medication. It's making me a little nervous. Can we talk about it? I don't know if it mixes well with your antidepressant, and I don't know if it might just be making your depression worse. Do you think we could speak to the doctor about it? Would you like me to go with you to your next appointment?" Deal with it in a gentle, collaborative way.

—DR. LAURA EPSTEIN ROSEN

I had an experience with depression several years ago and had a bad reaction to the medication I was given. My doctor has suggested that I might want to consider treatment again since my symptoms are returning. Is it possible that I might react differently to the medication, now that several years have passed, or will the reaction be the same?

If this was over a decade ago, most likely you were on the older generation medication, a tricyclic. Today your doctor would most likely prescribe a newer antidepressant with fewer side effects. Most side effects don't continue after the first couple of weeks on the treatment. If your doctor hadn't informed you of what they might be, it must have been upsetting. I find that when patients are alerted to possible problems and told that they will probably go away after a short while, it's usually not a big problem.

If you had an allergic reaction like a rash or difficulty breathing—which are unusual but possible problems—then be sure to talk to your doctor about exactly what happened last time and have him or her review all your options. It's possible you won't have the same reaction again, but it's not worth taking the chance. Your doctor will probably put you on a different medicine this time.

—DR. ROBERT HIRSCHFELD

Are antidepressant medications mind or personality altering?

Antidepressants tend to have a positive, helpful effect on personality: they stabilize your mood, increase your self-confidence and energy, and decrease your irritability. That's not a personality change. For a person who's had depression for 20 years, it may seem like a big shift, but it won't change that person in any fundamental way. If you didn't like avocados before, you're still not going to like them.

Antidepressant medications have an effect on the parts of the brain that are making you feel depressed. But they won't change the basic way you think. You will still be who you are. They are not cures; they merely reverse the processes that have caused your depression.

—DR. ROBERT HIRSCHFELD

Can a person become addicted to antidepressants?

Current research indicates that antidepressant medications are not addicting. The syndrome of addiction involves a need for continued increased use, regardless of harmful consequences. In the case of antidepressant medication, there is no such drive.

For recovering addicts, practitioners will often use caution in prescribing antidepressant medications—but not because of any potential for abuse or addiction. Rather, it's to avoid creating the sense of reward that someone with an addiction problem looks for when putting a substance into their system to feel better. An antidepressant, while not addictive, can make the patient feel significantly better, and therefore reinforce a behavior of searching for something to put into their system.

About 85 percent of addicts with depressive symptoms will get better with treatment for the addiction alone. Thus, there may be no role for antidepressant medication. For those who have an unresolved diagnosis of depression, antidepressants are an essential part of treatment—for the depression, and for the patient's recovery from addiction. If depressive symptoms go unchecked, the painful feelings would continue to drive the desire for escape and the addictive process.

—DR. DREW PINSKY

MEDICATION TREATMENT AND SIDE EFFECTS

> *Refer to the antidepressant medication chart on pages 104–105 for further information.*

What are the common side effects of antidepressant medications?

The older tricyclic medications, which have been available since the 1960s, affect chemicals in the brain related to depression, along with other receptors in the brain. Many of the common side effects related to the use of these medications occur because of the interaction of the drug with several receptors. Some of these side effects are: dry mouth, sleepiness, nervousness, constipation, and high overdose toxicity. Tricyclic antidepressants may also cause a fatal heart problem if taken in excess.

The class of antidepressants known as SSRIs may cause gastrointestinal side effects: nausea, diarrhea, gas, bloating. These problems are usually mild and can be lessened if you take the medication with a large glass of water and some food. Because they're better tolerated, patients are five to 10 percent less likely to stop taking them than tricyclics. There's also no danger to the heart, so they're safe should an accidental overdose occur.

Many antidepressants can cause sexual side effects. These may take the form of difficulty getting aroused, decreased desire, erectile problems and/or delayed ejaculation in men, decreased lubrication, and delayed or absent orgasm in women. Some of the newer medications, however, have a very low risk of these effects; these may include antidepressants from the norepinephrine dopamine reuptake inhibitor (NDRI), selective serotonin reuptake inhibitor and blocker (SSRIB), or tetracyclic classes.

Another class of drugs, called the monoamine oxidase inhibitors (MAOIs), have potential side effects such as weight gain, high or low blood pressure, and sexual dysfunction. This class can be dangerous if taken in combination with certain foods, or prescription or over-the-counter medications. For example, taking a cold pill or eating aged cheeses while on these antidepressants can cause a severe rise in blood pressure. MAOIs are often reserved for patients who have not responded to other antidepressants or who have what we call atypical features of depression: sleeping or eating too much, being overly sensitive to rejection, and feeling a sense of heaviness.

There are many sources of information about medications for clinical depression, such as the *Physicians' Desk Reference (PDR)*. You can also ask a pharmacist for package inserts that accompany medications about which you may have questions. Learn as much as you can about any medication your doctor prescribes.

—DR. DAVID DUNNER

My doctor wants to switch my antidepressant, but I have heard that some of them can cause weight gain. I feel bad enough as it is, without having to deal with gaining weight. Is there any way to avoid this?

Weight gain from antidepressants—defined as a seven percent gain over your usual weight—is the biggest concern of women patients. Yes, some antidepressants can cause you to gain weight, including any SSRI that you take for more than a year. Tetracyclics may cause weight gain, early in the treatment, and tricyclics and MAOIs may cause weight gain too.

If weight gain is a major concern to you, discuss it with your doctor and be sure he or she prescribes a medication that is not likely to cause this side effect.

Keep in mind, even if you're taking one of the medications that may cause weight gain, you have only about a 20 percent chance of having this side effect.

—Dr. Anita Clayton

Some antidepressants can cause you to gain weight. It can feel very sudden and upsetting. If this is a major concern to you, discuss it with your doctor up front. If you do gain weight as a result of your treatment, your doctor can try adding or switching to another antidepressant to fight this side effect. Exercise can help take the extra weight off, but some medications will resist even your best aerobic efforts. Strength training helps build muscle and speeds metabolism, which may help in weight control. You might also consider consulting a nutritionist. Don't take any over-the-counter (or prescribed) diet medications without the approval of the doctor who prescribed your antidepressant medication.

When I first became depressed, I wasn't eating and I lost weight. My husband called it "the depression diet." After I started taking one medication, I had an increased appetite and did gain weight. With the SSRIs you sometimes lose a little weight at first, but you can have a dramatic gain after about six months. This can be true with the antipsychotic and mood stabilizing medications, too. I gained 60 pounds in six months on a combination of antidepressants and mood stabilizers *without* feeling any increased appetite. I wished I could wear a sign to explain to people that I had ballooned up because of the medication: "It's not my fault!" Years later, I'm still trying to come to terms with a different body. For a lot of people, this side effect can be minimized, so talk to your doctor about your options.

—Dr. Martha Manning

I've noticed a strange sensation since I started taking antidepressant medication: I feel like I've just stepped off a roller coaster. I am dizzy all the time. Will this feeling go away with time?

Side effects that occur early are often temporary. But there are ways to handle those that are troublesome, such as changing the dose or adding another medication that eases the side effect, or trying behavioral techniques (drinking water if you're dizzy, for example). The worst thing you can do is to stop taking your medication on your own. It's best to talk to your doctor about the symptoms as you are experiencing them.

Be aware, though, that what can appear to be side effects are sometimes actually symptoms of depression: sleep difficulties, lack of energy, difficulty concentrating, exaggerated aches and pains. It's likely that you sought treatment when these symptoms were at their worst, so wait a few weeks and see if they disappear when the medication starts to work.

—Dr. David Dunner

I've been taking an antidepressant for a few months and I have been having trouble staying awake. (I sleep pretty much the whole day except when I'm at work.) What is happening to me?

It sounds like you need to talk to your doctor about changing the dose of your medication or switching to a different one. It's also possible that just switching the time of day you take the medication may solve the problem. Side effects usually occur within the first several hours, so if you're on a medication that makes you sleepy, taking it at night instead of in the morning may do the trick. If you're already taking it at night, then your doctor probably needs to adjust the dose. Switching to a medication that is less likely to cause drowsiness is another option for your doctor to consider.

—DR. ROBERT HIRSCHFELD

I recently started taking a medication for depression and I now wake up every night drenched in sweat—even when the weather is cool. Could this be related to the medication and is there any way to control it?

Sweating can be a side effect of some antidepressants. In some cases, the medications make your dreams extraordinarily vivid and colorful, which can lead to night sweats.

There's not much you can do about it except to keep the temperature in your bedroom cool and wear cotton nightclothes. If the sweating is so severe that you have to get out of bed once or twice a night to change your clothing, you should talk to your doctor about changing the medication or adding another medication to combat the sweating. (Women who may be approaching menopause must consider that menopause might be the cause of their night sweats.)

—DR. ANITA CLAYTON

What is the likelihood of getting sexual side effects from antidepressant medication?

It depends. The effect of serotonin contributes the most to sexual side effects, and 30 to 50 percent of people on one of the selective serotonin reuptake inhibitor (SSRI) medications may experience them. You'll be less likely to have sexual side effects if your doctor prescribes one of the newer antidepressant medications that fall in the NDRI, tetracyclic, or SSRIB classes.

The tricyclic medications and the MAOIs appear to present about the same likelihood of sexual side effects as the SSRIs.

Different medications act on certain phases of the sexual response cycle more than others. For example, the SSRIs seem more likely to cause problems related to orgasm or desire, less likely to cause problems with arousal. The older medications have a more overall effect on sexual functioning.

The percentage of people who suffer sexual side effects after taking antidepressants is fairly similar in women and men. But women are more likely to attribute these problems to changes in their relationship or to something in their own behavior, whereas men are more likely to state that their medication is causing the problem.

—DR. ANITA CLAYTON

Is there a difference between symptoms of sexual dysfunction caused by depression and symptoms of sexual dysfunction caused by the treatment of depression?

There are three main performance phases that define sexual function: desire, arousal, and release (ejaculation and orgasm). With depression, two of these—desire and arousal—may be impaired. With certain antidepressant medications, release may also be impaired. How the sexual problems express themselves is generally no different whether caused by depression or its treatment. But it's important to identify the cause of sexual problems because there are different ways of treating them.

If sexual problems are due to the illness itself, you will likely have experienced these problems before you started taking antidepressants. In this case, it's important to realize that sexual function may not return for a while even when your depression is properly treated. It's one of the last symptoms to return to normal. In addition, sometimes during depression and its recovery period, a couple has stopped being intimate with each other and has to learn how to regain this feeling. This requires time, patience, and sensitivity. For some, counseling can be very helpful too.

If the sexual problems occured after you began taking an antidepressant, it is more likely that the medication itself is the cause. Antidepressants in the SSRI category, the most commonly prescribed class of medications for this illness, may cause decreased sex drive, erectile problems, and delayed ejaculation in men, and decreased lubrication and delayed or absent orgasm in women. This is a result of the serotonin effect of these medications.

You need to let your doctor know if you experience any of these problems after starting an antidepressant. For people who are concerned about sexual side effects or have experienced them while taking an SSRI, other antidepressants are available that have low to no incidence of sexual side effects. You should work with your doctor to determine what options are best for you.

—Dr. David Dunner

My wife has had depression for many years and has not responded to medication. Her doctor suggested ECT treatment. I thought this treatment was no longer used. How does it work?

Many people feel surprised and frightened when ECT (electroconvulsive therapy) is recommended as a treatment option. Images from the 1940s and 1950s and graphic scenes from movies, such as *One Flew Over the Cuckoo's Nest,* have persisted in the public's consciousness. However, changes in the procedure have made it far more humane, much less traumatic, and extremely effective in the treatment of severe depression.

More and more, ECT is done on an outpatient basis when someone is able to deliver care and support at home. The procedure is fairly straightforward: general anesthesia and a strong muscle relaxant are given and, while a monitor tracks brain waves, a quick electric current is delivered which stimulates a brief seizure (unlike many other types of seizures, a seizure produced from ECT is self-limiting—it stops on its own). The patient emerges from the anesthesia shortly after, possibly with a headache or painful jaw.

A course of ECT usually involves six to 12 sessions and memory loss is the primary side effect; people may have difficulty remembering some events that occurred in the most recent past or during the time of treatment. However, research demonstrates that for most people, impaired memory abilities are passing and ECT does not affect memory for new information.

ECT is not a long-term treatment of depression and 50 percent of people who do not follow up with effective medication treatment will have a relapse. However, this does not diminish the importance of ECT. It seems to be able to break a seemingly inescapable cycle that occurs in resistant severe depression.

I have had two courses of ECT: I began sleeping more after my second treatment, I got some appetite back by the fourth. What was very interesting was that medicine that hadn't worked before worked after ECT. The second course of ECT was two years later, after I had refused adding a mood stabilizer to my treatment. Once again, ECT pulled me out of my depths, so that I could benefit from medicine and psychotherapy.

—DR. MARTHA MANNING

You read so much about St. John's wort. Is it safe for treating depression? Does it work?

While this dietary supplement has been reported in Europe as a safe and effective treatment for depression, there are potential dangers. Lack of U.S. government regulation has led to an inconsistency in the quantity of active ingredients in individual dosages. This inconsistency leaves consumers vulnerable because they can never be sure of what they are taking. Natural is not always synonymous with safe. The effectiveness of St. John's wort for the treatment of depression is currently being studied in the U.S.

St. John's wort has certain side effects that you should be aware of: the primary one is sensitivity to the sun while taking the herb. You should read the label for other precautions. In addition, you should never change your course of therapy without talking to your mental health professional. Only a qualified professional and the person with depression can make an informed decision about the best treatment options.

—DR. DAVID DUNNER

DEPRESSION IN MEN VERSUS WOMEN

Do men and women experience depression differently?

The description of symptoms does vary between women and men. In the past, trials of experimental medications for treating depression were usually done with men—for fear that if a woman taking an experimental medication became pregnant there would be a risk to the developing fetus. So what came to be seen as the "typical" symptoms of depression are really those that are typical for men: depressed mood, loss of interest or pleasure in activities, waking up too early in the morning and not being able to go back to sleep, loss of appetite leading to weight loss, decreased sex drive, problems with concentration or memory, and anger and irritability.

Women also tend to have depressed mood and loss of interest or pleasure in activities, but also have so-called "atypical" symptoms: too much sleep (up to 10 to 12 hours a night, and staying in bed even longer), increased appetite leading to weight gain, anxiety, problems with decision-making, guilt (especially about things they *failed* to do), and extreme sensitivity to rejection.

—DR. ANITA CLAYTON

I'm being treated for depression, and I would like to get pregnant. Do I need to go off my medication before trying? If not, once becoming pregnant, do I need to stop taking the medication?

Antidepressant medications have not been found to cause birth defects. However, it's a good idea to limit an unborn baby's exposure to all drugs. Your doctor may advise you to go off your medication very gradually before getting pregnant. If your symptoms recur, you'll need to decide with your doctor whether or not to start the medication again. If you do go back on the antidepressant, you can decide whether to stop again once you get pregnant—and/or to try psychotherapy.

Some women unexpectedly become pregnant while on antidepressant medications, and may decide to go off them. About 10 percent of women develop depression during pregnancy, sometimes for the first time. These women usually need treatment, with talk therapy or with medication. Another option to consider and speak with your doctor about is the use of light therapy to treat depression during pregnancy.

We don't know much about any possible long-term behavioral effects on a child whose mother took antidepressants while pregnant or while breastfeeding. That's why it's probably best to taper off your medications if possible. However, if your depression goes untreated there can be negative effects on your baby, before and after birth. You have to weigh all the risks and benefits, the severity of the illness, and your response to any past treatment, then work with your doctor to decide on the best course of action.

—Dr. Anita Clayton

I had a baby a few months ago and since then I have been feeling down. I have no interest in being physically close with my husband, and I feel guilty that my baby is not bringing me any joy. My doctor suggested trying an antidepressant. Is that really necessary or will this go away? If it will go away, when will that be?

Depression often appears in the postpartum period. The first thing you might want to think about is how much help you have in taking care of your baby. If you're doing all the child care alone and are exhausted, that could be the problem. Are you nursing? Are you up two or three times a night to feed the baby? If your problem is mainly one of exhaustion, try to get your husband to help with the feedings and anything else you can think of that would allow you to get more rest. If you already have a support system, however, the problem is more likely to be depression.

A lot of factors could contribute to a new mother's "feeling down." You may have older children with different but very demanding needs. You may have a husband who is not interacting with your newborn the way you need or expect him to. Your weight is probably higher than before you got pregnant, and you may be feeling less attractive. All of these things may make you shy away from being physically close with your husband.

One way your doctor can determine whether you are indeed clinically depressed is to find out whether you have a family history of depression, or whether you yourself have ever had a previous episode. If you're not depressed, your symptoms should lift within a couple of weeks.

As far as feeling guilty that you're not experiencing joy about your baby, this could also be from extreme fatigue. A major mood disorder would not be suspected unless this went on for several weeks and showed symptoms like sadness, sleep disturbances, and lack of interest not only in your baby but in other things you used to enjoy. And, unlike the much more common "baby blues," postpartum depression doesn't begin right away, but two to four weeks after the baby's birth.

If you are diagnosed with depression and you're a nursing mother, it is important to know that antidepressant medication will be passed into your breast milk. We don't know a lot about what the effect on the baby might be, but we know that some antidepressants are safer than others when nursing. If your doctor prescribes a different medication for you, you might be advised to stop nursing. Keep in mind that the drug will be present in the greatest amounts in breast milk five to seven hours after you take it, so you may be able to manage if you work around that.

It's of crucial importance to get help. Your symptoms will not necessarily go away on their own. The early bonding experience will be profoundly affected if you are not emotionally available to your baby. And you deserve to see your symptoms relieved rather than just suffer through them.

—DR. THOMAS WISE

Are men or women more likely to experience sexual side effects from antidepressant treatments?

We don't know. Women have more trouble reaching orgasm—but it's important to know whether there was a problem before they started taking the medication. A woman may have lubrication problems too, but that could be because of a lowered sex drive.

Men's problems will be with delayed orgasm, not an inability to have orgasm. They may experience erectile difficulties, too. The research on how many will have these problems is not consistent. From 30 up to 80 percent may have suffered these side effects from the older tricyclic drugs. Early studies with the SSRIs did not ask very detailed or specific questions, so the extremely low incidence of reported sexual side effects was not reliable.

Further questionnaire-type studies revealed that about one-third experienced sexual side effects, and when men were asked directly, 96 percent admitted experiencing them. You can see it's a very common problem. Unfortunately, a lot of the testing was conducted with male patients only, so we have less information about the effects on women.

—DR. THOMAS WISE

That's hard to say. Men and women don't differ much in their responses when asked. But men are more likely to attribute a sexual problem to the medication and to report it to their doctors, whereas women may need to be asked about it directly.

Women may appear to experience more sexual side effects partly because they're more likely than men already to have had difficulties with sexual function. So if a doctor asks a woman on antidepressant medication whether she's been having trouble getting aroused, for example, she may say yes without explaining that this is nothing new.

—DR. ANITA CLAYTON

I find when I'm feeling depressed I have trouble getting—and keeping—an erection. Is this normal? Should I consider stopping the medication I am on?

Depression may impair a man's ability to get a full erection. More commonly, men will have a lowered sex drive, so they may not enjoy sex as much. Furthermore, erectile dysfunction can often be caused by anxiety or by the antidepressant medication they're taking. Don't stop taking your medication. Talk to your doctor about how to solve the problem. He or she may decide to add to or switch the medication after discussing the problem with you.

—DR. THOMAS WISE

Help! I am 42, going through menopause, very depressed, and have zero sexual desire. I have tried many antidepressants but because of the combination of hormones and antidepressants, the side effects are too severe, not to mention that they make my lack of libido even worse. I'm in a new relationship and have a very understanding mate, but our sex life is nonexistent and it's taking a toll on both of us. Any help for menopausal women who are also suffering from depression?

You have several possibilities, so don't give up hope. One would be to try a different hormone replacement therapy. (Interestingly, some women in the early stages of menopause who are not on hormone replacement therapy will respond better to the antidepressant if hormone replacement therapy is added.) Be aware, too, that your low sex drive could be from the menopause and/or the depression itself.

As you go through menopause, your body decreases its production of estrogen, progesterone, and testosterone. Women have a lot less testosterone in their bodies than men do, but it's important to a woman's sex drive. In fact, some hormone replacement therapies contain both estrogen and testosterone to help keep up a woman's sexual desire.

Other possible remedies would be for your doctor to add a second antidepressant to help maintain your feelings of sexual desire.

Other strategies sometimes help the antidepressant work better. For example, taking thyroid medication or a mood stabilizer may be of help. Talk with your doctor about all your options so you can help him or her zero in on the right combination. You don't have to deny yourself a sexual relationship with the new man in your life.

—DR. ANITA CLAYTON

CHAPTER 3

RELATIONSHIP ISSUES: DEALING WITH DEPRESSION TOGETHER

HELPING YOURSELF OR YOUR PARTNER IDENTIFY AND GET TREATED FOR DEPRESSION

Lately, my partner is moody, distant, and emotionally withdrawn. Could she have depression?

Yes. We all have our ups and downs, but if her symptoms persist for more than two weeks, depression would be a strong possibility. As you have probably noticed, depression can have a negative effect on relationships. A depressed person becomes emotionally unavailable, dependent, and different from the person you're used to. Help your partner by urging her to talk to her doctor about it.

—Dr. Robert Hirschfeld

How do I help my partner? He refuses treatment for his depression even though his doctor is recommending it. He thinks he needs to go through the experience of the depression.

It's so hard to watch someone you love in pain and refusing to get help. He may feel he needs to suffer—this is a symptom of his depression. Don't take it personally.

Set aside a quiet time to have a conversation about it—not during an argument or when one of you is rushing off to work. Be direct and compassionate. Tell him you've noticed that he doesn't seem like himself lately, and that you think he might have depression. Tell him you'd like him to get treatment so that he can feel better. Say that

45

you've read that if depression goes untreated, the episodes may become more severe and more frequent. For some people, this is all you'll need to do. Your partner may be relieved that you've noticed the problem and that you're giving him a push to do something about it. It might take several conversations over the course of a few weeks to get to this point.

In other cases, the person will resist. If this happens with your partner, try to convince him gently that he doesn't have to go through this agony. Say that he may as well try to get help—nothing could make him feel worse than he already does. One way that's often effective is to ask the person to do this for *you*. Tell him it's troubling you to see him so upset. Offer him pamphlets or books about depression in the hope that he will pick them up and read them. Sometimes a person isn't familiar enough with what depression looks like to recognize it in himself.

If you think it might help, you could hold a small gathering of his family and/or friends and take turns talking to him about your concerns. Only you know him well enough to determine whether this would be effective or just make him defensive.

Tread lightly until you find a way that works. The exception would be if your partner starts talking about killing himself, or about to whom he wants to leave various possessions. Then you must get immediate help—no matter how much he resists. Get him to an emergency room or dial 911. More than 15 percent of people with untreated or undertreated depression take their own lives—*any mention of suicide must be taken seriously.*

—Dr. Laura Epstein Rosen

About 30 years ago, a popular belief sprang up that depression was a "growth experience" and that dealing with the pain of it was a good thing. That kind of thinking is less common today, but there are people, like your partner, who still feel this way. There's no evidence that going through the experience of depression is beneficial in any way. In fact, the longer you stay depressed, the less able you will be to deal with its effects. Depression clouds your judgment, saps your energy and motivation, and makes you feel pessimistic—as though nothing will be able to help you, and it's your fate to suffer through it.

—DR. ROBERT HIRSCHFELD

Should I recommend couples therapy to my husband to help him with his depression? He's so withdrawn, he doesn't even realize it's affecting our marriage.

I'm a strong supporter of couples therapy as an important part of treating depression—often in addition to medication and/or individual psychotherapy. Depression can have a devastating effect on relationships. Marriages in which one partner has untreated depression are nine times more likely than others to end in divorce. The number one reason couples seek couples therapy is because of a sexual problem; in half of those cases, the problem can be traced to depression in one of them. Furthermore, you're four times more likely to become depressed yourself if you live with a depressed person. You're apt to resent him for making you overcompensate for the damage it's doing to the relationship. You desperately need to break the cycle.

Couples therapy will open the door and provide a safe place to speak openly. The focus will be on the relationship, not on the person. This will help your husband understand that it's not his fault. If he refuses to consider couples therapy, try to get him at least to agree to a consultation, or to letting you come with him to a session with his own therapist. If none of these approaches work, you may want to consider individual therapy for yourself—you need support, too, when your husband has depression.

—DR. LAURA EPSTEIN ROSEN

You're right that something definitely needs to be done. If your spouse is depressed, couples therapy can be helpful. For a good number of couples currently in therapy together, one of the spouses is clinically depressed. If you feel the marriage is being affected, then it would definitely be useful for both of you to be seen.

The only exception I would make is that if this is his first episode, and early in his treatment, you might want to hold off on couples therapy to give the antidepressant time to do its work. For at least 80 percent of patients, treatment will be successful within a couple of months.

—Dr. David Dunner

My wife has been in talk therapy for at least four years. For a while it seemed like it was really working, I'm not sure it still is. I'd like to suggest that she speak with her doctor about getting medication prescribed. How do I initiate this conversation in such a way that she doesn't become defensive?

It's natural for you to have these questions and concerns about your wife's treatment. The best thing for you to do would be to pick a specific time to talk to her about it—not in the middle of another conversation or when you're rushed. Say, "At first I thought your therapy was working, but now I'm not so sure. What do you think?" Focus on what you feel, and talk in a collaborative way about the problem. Suggest that you might come along to a session with her to discuss your concerns with her therapist.

Encourage your wife to learn about all treatment possibilities. People vary. Some are more comfortable with talk therapy only, some with medication only, some with both. If she gets defensive, drop it and bring it up another time. I have found with married couples that, if one partner feels strongly about the other one trying another treatment option, the person with depression will often do it. Try your best, but there's only so much you can do. Help your wife learn more about her options, but realize you'll have to respect her decision in the end.

—Dr. Laura Epstein Rosen

There's so much stigma attached to having depression. How can I stop my partner from being ashamed of my illness?

48

You can't stop your partner from feeling *anything*, so don't even try. But you can try to understand how to define what the "stigma" is. Is it shame? Fear of others finding out? These notions fit in perfectly with your own thoughts when you're depressed, and they can paralyze you.

Try to get your partner to describe how the stigma feels to him or her—if it feels lousy, then why it's lousy. Mental illness and being overweight are the two things that seem okay to make fun of in the popular media. How could we not feel stigmatized? I've been talking about and dealing with depression for 10 years, and I still feel the stigma with others.

It always helps to join forces. People who suffer from HIV are a great example. They mobilized to destigmatize their illness, and successfully turned around many popular perceptions. Get involved in your local National DMDA group or with your community mental health center.

Once when I was waiting at a crowded pharmacy counter for a medication to be refilled, a new assistant behind the counter yelled out, "Manning? Do you want that lithium with a childproof lid?" Part of me told myself I had nothing to be ashamed of. But the other part of me wanted to crawl under a rock. People were looking at me. The stigma is real.

—DR. MARTHA MANNING

There is no doubt that there is still a stigma attached to depression. One purpose of this book is to chip away at that stigma and give people a better understanding of depression by showing you how this illness can be managed—especially within relationships.

It is most unfortunate that people suffer further because of society's general misunderstanding about the nature of this disease. Historically, public attitudes toward depression have often been terribly uninformed, unfair, cruel, and outright ignorant. A person suffering from depression is no less worthwhile because of his or her condition than is someone suffering from heart disease or cancer.

If, in spite of reasonable reassurances, your partner continues to have intense shame, you might want to invite him or her to join you for couples therapy to work through this situation. It is something that can generally be substantially improved through the therapeutic process. Another suggestion is to attend a National DMDA support group. If your husband can talk with members of other families, he will realize he is not alone. This should help lessen his feelings of shame.

—DR. DREW PINSKY

HELPING YOURSELF OR YOUR PARTNER THROUGH SEXUAL DYSFUNCTION

My partner no longer seems interested in me sexually. I don't know if it is because of his depression or not, but I am hurt and frustrated. What can I do, and how can I talk to him about this?

Depression can certainly lower a person's interest in sex. The feelings of fatigue, unattractiveness, and overall negativity may make sexual activity seem like just too much effort. Some patients describe their depression as a feeling of "walking through molasses all day." And low sex drive itself is one of the symptoms of depression.

The first thing you can do is realize that your initial response to the problem may not be the best one. Many partners of people with depression wind up lashing out at them or making them feel guilty for not being able to perform sexually. Have realistic expectations: your partner may not be interested in sex right now, and it may take some time for your sex life to get back to normal. (Many couples tell me that after one of them is treated for depression, their sex lives are actually better than before the depression began.)

Second, offer your support. If he's feeling worthless and unattractive, let him know you find him attractive. Touch him without the expectation that it will end in sex. Keep the physical connection going in an unthreatening way by just cuddling and hugging. Be patient. Let him know you'll be there when he feels ready.

Third, share your feelings with him. Let him know that you're concerned about the changes in your sex life and that you miss the physical closeness of it. Try to use "I" statements—"I miss your touch," "I feel rejected and unattractive when you don't want to have sex"—rather than put the problem in terms of him.

Fourth, try not to take his disinterest in sex personally. Understand that it's a symptom of his depression.

Lastly, ask for help. Speak to his doctor, if your partner agrees. If he's taking an antidepressant medication that might be causing sexual side effects, there are alternatives. However, his doctor must be informed of the problem.

—DR. LAURA EPSTEIN ROSEN

I've recently been diagnosed as having clinical depression. My doctor suggested putting me on an antidepressant medication, but I told him I wasn't sure about it and would get back to him. I've heard from several of my friends that some—maybe all—medications can seriously affect my libido. I am a newlywed, and enjoy a very good sexual relationship with my husband. I don't want to lose that. What do I do? Stay depressed and have a sex life or feel better and make my husband miserable?

Depression itself often causes problems with sexual desire and performance, and antidepressants can often get one's sex drive back to normal. However, there are certain medications that can bring on sexual problems. It's great that you enjoy a good sexual relationship with your husband. If you do wind up on an antidepressant that affects your sex life, don't mistake it as a personal statement of your feelings for each other. As with anything in a marriage, good communication is the first step. Let your husband know that you've noticed changes in your sexual desire and/or performance and that you will speak to your doctor about it. Encourage your husband not to take it personally and to work with you on it.

Speak openly with your doctor about your concerns, and about taking one of the antidepressant medications with a low likelihood of sexual side effects (see medication chart on pages 104–105). If any sexual side effects do appear, there are things that can be done, like changing the dosage, changing the time of day when you take the medication, or adding another antidepressant to get rid of the side effects of the first. Or you could be treated without medication, using psychotherapy.

—DR. LAURA EPSTEIN ROSEN

From my perspective, not treating the depression may actually be more of a risk to your sexual relations than the potential side effects of the medication. It sounds like your relationship is still quite connected emotionally, so this may be an opportunity to treat your biological mood-state and reduce the risk of future relationship problems, which might otherwise occur.

—DR. DREW PINSKY

My husband is currently being treated for depression. His mood has improved but his medication interferes with our sex life. He wants to quit the medication. I am afraid he'll become depressed again. What can I do?

Today, no one has to choose between suffering with sexual side effects or remaining depressed. It is essential for your husband to continue his medication, or his depression may well recur. The doctor may decide to switch to a different antidepressant that doesn't interfere with your sex life, or to add a second one to lessen these effects. There are solutions, depending on what the problem is.

SSRIs, for example, can treat premature ejaculation, though they can also cause erectile dysfunction and absence of orgasm. Other classes of medication such as NDRI, tetracyclic, or SSRIB are very effective in counteracting sexual side effects, except for delayed ejaculation. Different people respond differently to medications. It might take some time to find the right one, or the right combination, for your husband, so try to be patient. Urge your husband to communicate clearly with his doctor and to not end his treatment without his doctor's approval.

—DR. THOMAS WISE

I am taking medication for my bipolar disorder and my sex drive is almost nonexistent. I have been married nearly three years, am 26 and miserable. How can I get my sex life back? My husband is supportive, but frustrated.

The first thing you need to do is find out whether your low sex drive is due to the medication, the bipolar disorder itself, or a hormonal imbalance. Discuss the problem with your doctor so he or she can make a diagnosis and any necessary adjustments to your medication.

—DR. DAVID DUNNER

My husband has been taking antidepressant medication for three months. I have noticed a miraculous change. He is feeling better, working again, and attending our children's extracurricular activities like he used to. The only problem is he has no interest in sex. I am afraid to say something to him, because he is really feeling like his old self in so many other ways. Help!

The worst you can do is to say nothing. If you're afraid that your husband will stop the medication, or will feel ashamed, then say something like, "I read an article about a man who was taking antidepressants and feeling great but lost his sex drive. There's something that can be done about it." Also, talking about sex with your doctor may be uncomfortable but it's really necessary. If your husband agrees, go with him to talk to his doctor. Find out what can be done, like changing to another medication or adding a different medication to the one he is already taking.

Managing a sexual problem involves assessing many factors. Had your husband been interested in sex before? Are there any issues between the two of you that helped or hindered his sexual functioning? Are there any other medical problems that might be causing his disinterest in sex? Any history of substance abuse? All these things are possible factors that you'll need to discuss with your doctor.

—DR. THOMAS WISE

It's great that your husband is feeling so much better. It must be a huge relief to both of you. After three months on antidepressant medication most of his symptoms should be lessened, but it's possible that his lack of interest in sex could be a lingering symptom of the depression. Are any of his other depressive symptoms still obvious—feelings of worthlessness, fatigue, sleeping or eating problems?

Your husband should speak to his doctor about the possibility of sexual side effects from his medication. I've heard someone describe it as feeling like her "sexual light bulb had dimmed." If this is what's causing your husband's problem, the doctor can change the dosage or switch to a medication that is less likely to cause sexual side effects. If you're nervous about bringing this up to your husband, tread carefully and choose a relaxed moment (not when you're making love). Let him know that you're on his side. Offer to go to the doctor with him. Tell him you're thrilled with the positive changes in him, but that you're sad because you miss the physical aspect of your relationship.

—DR. LAURA EPSTEIN ROSEN

I am currently taking a medication that works well for me, but I have lost my sexual desire. My wife and I have decided to have a second child. Do you have any advice for us?

Antidepressant medication does not cause sterility. If you are functioning sexually, you can father another child. If you can't get an erection, see your doctor and find out ways to restore function. If your antidepressant is working well, don't go off it without talking with your doctor. It's great that you have a positive outlook and want another child!

—DR. THOMAS WISE

Do you have any advice for someone experiencing depression who is also just starting a relationship and trying to become intimate?

It's very important to communicate with your partner about your illness. Educate your partner thoroughly so he or she will not blame

54

either of you for the potential symptoms that could appear as a result of your depression. Reassure your partner that you are interested in intimacy, and explain to him or her how your depression may cause you to withdraw from that interest, or at times make you a less than enthusiastic partner. Encourage, if your partner is open to this, participation in your treatment plan wherever possible.

—DR. DREW PINSKY

DEALING WITH THE STRAIN ON YOUR EMOTIONAL INTIMACY

I'm feeling more like myself since starting treatment for depression, but my relationship is still not the same. How can I feel close to my husband again?

This is a tricky question. The partner of a person with depression often experiences a good deal of distress too, and in order to manage those feelings, he or she withdraws from the patient. Your husband may find himself withdrawn or defensive, perhaps not trusting that your symptoms have been relieved. This is, of course, the very opposite of what you and your husband need.

It's very important for your husband to learn about depression, not blame himself, not feel hurt or less worthwhile, and not become angry and disconnected from you as you recover. Certainly these feelings are normal, but your husband needs to be encouraged to hang in as you begin to get well.

You may also feel uneasy in the relationship if you are concerned that your feelings may return to depression. You may be reluctant to be vulnerable or intimate for fear of being hurt or feeling anxious— maybe triggering the unpleasant feeling you just got past.

It may be helpful to ask your husband to participate in couples therapy, where feelings and fears can be expressed in a safe manner. This can make a difference in your ultimate recovery from depression and the survival of your relationship.

It's a difficult challenge, and it takes a great deal of trust and self-awareness. Reestablishing intimacy is an essential part of human happiness, and extremely important for the treatment of depression.

—DR. DREW PINSKY

Relationship problems and depression do not appear or get better overnight. Depression packs a powerful punch, even on strong relationships. Recovery is somewhat uneven—you may get your energy back but still feel negative and low. Try to approach the process by thinking about it in steps. Think of simple ways you can be together, like going to a movie or taking a walk. Work up to restoring all aspects of the relationship, such as shared interests, trust, family activities, and physical intimacy.

Keep in mind that it's normal for a relationship to be impacted by depression, and it takes some time to get it back, just like it would from any other personal challenge.

The medications I first took for my depression didn't cause sexual dysfunction. But then I stopped responding to any medications, and as I became more and more depressed, I grew less interested in sex, to the point where I hated being touched. I grew more and more distant from my husband as he clearly became my caretaker. After I was hospitalized and tried different combinations of medications, I felt much better. I still didn't want to have sex, but at least I could recognize those feelings. I had a good doctor who validated for me that it was a side effect of the medications, and not something wrong with me.

With that sexless feeling, you're like a robot and it can be very hurtful to your partner. You remember what sex is, but you think, "Why would I want to do that?" My husband and I were very shaken by what we went through. Problems with arousal and orgasm can be very long term. We've learned to enjoy things like massaging and cuddling without necessarily progressing to sex. He came with me to my doctor appointments to help clarify that it wasn't the depression or our marriage or him. It was the medication.

—DR. MARTHA MANNING

What can be done for people who have depression, believe they don't deserve to be intimate, and feel that it is impossible to be intimate until their depression is lessened?

Some of the strongest symptoms of depression deal with feeling worthless, unlovable, and unattractive. These are not symptoms that can be reasoned away. Gently remind your partner of how much you love them and how special they are to you. List the qualities you like about the person, and let them know you don't blame them. Don't come on too strong, though. Have realistic expectations and respect the person's need for distance. A depressed person will often turn down offers of support—saying they need space or that you're nagging, for example.

It is difficult but possible to help someone through this period. Stay involved even when you're not getting the reaction you want. Help the person understand that you're there to help, and try not to take it personally if he or she doesn't want your help. Be patient.

—DR. LAURA EPSTEIN ROSEN

My mom and I lost our "connection" a long time ago. I am sure she is depressed, but she's never been diagnosed with depression, and is afraid to go to a psychiatrist. I know she will never get better unless she takes this first step. How do I help her to do this?

This is a common, difficult, and tricky problem. You're right: your mother probably will not get better unless she "takes this first step." You should be aware, however, that depression is diagnosed quite routinely by primary care physicians, who can also prescribe antidepressant medication when appropriate. This means that most primary care doctors are trained to assess someone like your mother and make a determination of whether there is a diagnosis of depression.

You also should be aware that, particularly in older people, other medical problems can lead to and/or actually cause depression. Perhaps you could take that approach with your mother—reassuring her that you're concerned about her health and pointing out some of

57

the symptoms you have noticed—to get her to see her primary care physician. You could accompany your mother to her doctor's appointment and share your observations with him or her, if your mother agrees. Or you could contact her doctor before or after the visit to express what you've been observing so the doctor can make a more thorough assessment of your mother's condition.

If depression is diagnosed, her physician would probably initiate and monitor antidepressant therapy. I'd also recommend psychotherapy, if appropriate. If, later on, a psychiatrist was needed, the primary care doctor would be in a much better position to refer your mother to an appropriate professional, having established a trusting relationship with her.

—DR. DREW PINSKY

As the partner of someone with depression, I'm curious about the difference between depression and personality. Sometimes it is hard to remember that this irritable, difficult person is the person I love.

Personality is usually defined as the longstanding traits that appear in childhood and stay with you through life. Depression is a temporary mood state, even if the depression has existed for a long time. As hard as it can be to separate the symptoms of depression from the personality of someone you love, it will help you if you can do so. She is not her depression, and her behavior toward you is not intentional. Once the depression is treated, you will have your partner back and you'll realize how much of the irritability and withdrawal was caused by the depression.

—DR. LAURA EPSTEIN ROSEN

I'd like to get some information about the powerlessness and the patience of partners. What can we do to help ourselves and our partners who are suffering?

My husband and I call it "switching to paper plates." You need to learn to simplify life for a while. Understand that it's going to be a difficult period. Child care may be the most important issue to deal with. If people offer to help, ask for concrete things like giving your child a ride to school or afterschool activities. That will temporarily relieve you of at least one responsibility. Aside from that, you can seek out support groups. Educate yourself about depression. Go to the doctor with your partner. Continue your usual activities; don't let your partner's depression consume you. Gain control through your understanding and knowledge about the illness. Knowledge is greatly comforting.

As for patience, that's a tough one. For many people with depression, it's a long fight. You may start out as a saint in your efforts to help your partner through it, but those batteries are going to run down fast. Try not to get sucked into your partner's negativity. It's very important and not the slightest bit selfish to keep your regular life going as much as possible. You'll need those reality checks outside of your relationship. Do everything you can to normalize your life so that you can ward off depression in yourself and keep yourself in the best shape to help your partner.

—Dr. Martha Manning

I'm interested in knowing about partners who feel a profound sense of loss for the depressed person in their lives, and the emotional journey that they go through in terms of missing their partner.

Depression robs its victims of the best weapon for fighting it: themselves. The self often goes underground in a siege of depression, leaving them without tools to fight the illness. Living with a person with depression can mean living with a ghost.

Partners of people with depression commonly feel loss as well as fear that the person they love might not come back. The partners also feel angry, which is hard to deal with because they know the person they love is hurting. The burden falls on the healthy partner to take up the slack—to deal with the depressed partner's missed work, for example, creating further stress.

You must both keep in mind that, with treatment, your partner will get better *gradually*. There may be patterns of improvement, then regression. There will be leftover feelings and issues that will need to be dealt with. For example, when a hurricane hits, the immediate reaction is, "Thank God we're safe." Then, a bit later you say: "Look at this mess!" Once the person with depression is getting better, then the partner will be better able to express his or her feelings.

Support groups can be invaluable. My husband now wishes he had joined one during my own depression. They can validate your feelings and take you out of your isolation. Unlike with other illnesses—when people often offer to cook a meal or mow your lawn—friends and neighbors don't tend to give practical help. My husband used to say, "There are no depression casseroles." No one on the outside is going to be able to sympathize as much as those who have "been there." My husband went through a terrible time, not only because I was "gone" but because he couldn't be sure I was "coming back." He did a lot of hovering over me, checking on me. He had all the added responsibility of dealing with our household and daughter. His anger erupted later, when I was able to handle it. He was hesitant to share his feelings with his family or friends, which made the burden on him much heavier. Allow yourself to share your problems. You can't get help if people don't know you need it.

—DR. MARTHA MANNING

How do I get through the difficult times when my partner has no energy, never wants to go out, and can't stand to be with others? Why should my life suffer because of his depression?

Feeling sympathy for a depressed person we love sometimes makes us want to give up our own needs. This is a mistake. It could even make you become depressed yourself. It can also increase your feelings of resentment and frustration toward your partner.

Make an effort to keep up with most of your usual activities and diversions—go to parties, go to the gym, go shopping. They will keep you refreshed and better equipped to help your partner. Invite your partner to join you, but respect his decision if he says no. Try not to criticize him for being a couch potato. Tell him you're disappointed that he's not going with you, and ask him whether it's all right with him if you go alone. You might want to take a friend instead, or plan on coming home early. Explain that although you know he really isn't up to the event, you'll feel sad if you don't go and that it's important for you to hold on to some of your usual activities.

Just remember that he won't be like this forever. If he's getting the proper treatment, he should be feeling more energetic soon. In the meantime, you shouldn't give up everything in your life.

—Dr. Laura Epstein Rosen

My marriage is falling apart. My husband has depression and is taking medication, but I can't get through to him. I've started therapy myself, but I still don't feel like it is getting any better for us. What more can we do? We have been married for over 15 years and I don't want to divorce, but am feeling helpless at this point.

It's hard to be the partner of a person with depression. If it goes on for an extended period of time, the relationship changes dramatically, and you may feel sad or worn down with the feeling that you're "losing" your husband because he's not able to do the things he used to do. It's not easy to maintain the effort it takes to stay close to him. The most important thing is to reestablish a connection and to learn how to change your expectations and your behavior. Couples therapy could help significantly with these goals. It would be a safe place for the two of you to talk about the strain that your husband's depression is putting on your marriage.

—Dr. Anita Clayton

When someone is suffering from a terrible depression and doesn't want to talk, how can I communicate with him or her? How do I break through? How do I say, "I'm here," if he or she doesn't want to talk?

This is quite a challenge, and patience on your part may be the most important contribution you can offer. At times it's simply not possible for someone who has depression to reach out and communicate. "Breaking through" may not be important to the person suffering from the depression. However, your presence, support, and concern are always needed and appreciated, although they may not always seem to be. When you need to talk to your partner, understand that that is *your* need. When you need him or her to respond in a certain way to your overtures, that is again *your* need. It may not coincide with theirs. If they don't want to talk, hearing you say, "I'm here" is often sufficient. If you are genuinely empathic and available, I assure you that when they can communicate more clearly, they will.

—DR. DREW PINSKY

Talking about feelings is difficult for someone with depression. It has little to do with your skill at breaking through and much to do with the grip of the illness on the person. How well the person communicated with you prior to the illness has nothing to do with how they will communicate now. The two of you will regain your ability to communicate as the depression is treated, but in the meantime figure out together what works and what doesn't. Some people develop a simple system of signals—like "Do you want a hug or not?" or "Do you want me in the same room with you or not?" Don't get into a big struggle.

Just being *with* the person, participating in the treatment, helping with the basics, are very important things to do. You're not the doctor or the therapist. All you can do is try to get back to basics with them. And get them to a doctor. During my depression I'd say to my husband, Brian, who's also a therapist, "Just be my husband. Don't try to be my doctor." It can ease your partner's tendency to be a caretaker to hear you say, "Sit with me, put your arm around me. Don't do any more than that."

—DR. MARTHA MANNING

Since I was diagnosed with depression a few months ago, my boyfriend tiptoes around me. I think he believes that he is the cause of my depression. How can I make him understand that it isn't anything he is saying or doing—it is me?

It's hard to be close to someone and *not* feel responsible for their depression. People with depression bring their darkness with them. Your partner has to deal with this and often with your irritability, and in so doing may feel that it's his fault. It's no surprise that in at least 50 percent of couples who seek therapy together, one of the partners has depression: people tend to blame the relationship before they think of depression as being the cause of the problem.

To complicate things, professionals have not always been welcoming of partners; or, if the partner does want to be involved, he or she is sometimes made to feel blame. Actually the partner is one of the cornerstones of treatment. Since depression often negatively affects memory and involves distortions in thinking, the partner can give another perspective to the therapist. Also, your boyfriend can help put the recommendations from the session into use. With your permission, your doctor should have an open-door policy toward your boyfriend, both to understand the person closest to you and to better assess the change that is taking place as treatment progresses.

If your boyfriend sees the doctor with you, he might be able to participate in getting you well. For example, if you say to the doctor, "I'm not anxious," and your boyfriend says, "You're always pacing the floor and wringing your hands," this is a valuable perspective.

—DR. MARTHA MANNING

Depression affects mood, sleep, appetite, motivation—and other people. It puts tremendous stress on close relationships and can easily lead to arguments and misunderstandings. Some partners respond by attempting to liven the person up or even picking a fight, thinking they can snap the person out of it.

Others, like your boyfriend, withdraw. This is his way of coping. His intentions are good—he doesn't want to upset you, he just wants you to be more like your old self—but you probably find the behavior frustrating. You may be angry that he's not being himself and is treating you too carefully. The solution? Talk to him about it. Teach him that he's not to blame for your depression and that he should stop feeling responsible and just treat you normally. Tell him your depression is not about him.

Then try to come up with ways in which he *can* be helpful to you. He can't read your mind. Tell him clearly and precisely that you'd like him to understand when you don't feel like going out, to give you some space, to give you a hug at the end of a long day—whatever you can think of that might make you feel a little better and give him some way to feel that he is helping. When you're feeling irritable and you find yourself snapping at him, try to let him know that it's not because of him, but that you're just feeling awful that day.

—DR. LAURA EPSTEIN ROSEN

I'm only 19 and I have had depression for many years. I've never been in a relationship and I worry about getting close with someone. How difficult will it be for me to find someone to be intimate with? And is there something I can do to make sure I am not pushing away potential relationships?

At 19 it's normal to be preoccupied about getting "close with someone." Not everyone is lucky enough to have a close and intimate relationship during this time, but eventually most people do. Depression makes it more difficult to connect with somebody. And there's no doubt that depression during adolescence significantly affects one's ability to carry on stable, healthy relationships. It's very difficult to add the stress of an interpersonal relationship when it's already so hard to manage the activities of daily living. However, in no way should you expect that this important experience is not open to you. In fact, it's an important part of recovery from depression.

One vital step is to make sure you are receiving appropriate treatment for your depression. This will decrease any feelings of irritability and withdrawal, and improve the likelihood that you'll have the energy and the desire to seek intimacy. It will also decrease the chance that you'll be pushing potential relationships away.

I also believe that talk therapy is an important part of treatment. The support of a therapist can increase your capacity to take risks and to tolerate disappointment. It can even provide a model for a healthy relationship for you to use as you pursue relationships with your peers.

—DR. DREW PINSKY

WHEN YOU BOTH SUFFER FROM DEPRESSION

Both my partner and I suffer from major depression. He has bipolar disorder. I have a hard time dealing with his depression, and he has a hard time dealing with my depression. What should we do?

Depressed people tend to marry other depressed people, so your problem is more common than you may think. The first thing is to get both of you as well as possible.

Relationships are very hard when you're depressed. Work with your doctor to manage your symptoms of depression. Once both your moods are more stable, the relationship will benefit. Couples therapy is an option, once your worst symptoms are under control. Participation in a National DMDA support group can provide insight into how other couples deal with their illnesses. When you have depression you can lose sight of how it affects the other people in your life. The fact that you two seem aware of this is already a good sign.

—DR. DAVID DUNNER

PARTNERS AND DEPRESSION

- Maintaining intimacy with a partner during depression may be difficult, but with open communication intimacy can grow
- Including your partner in all aspects of the recovery process is key to restoring intimacy
- Psychotherapy, individually and as a couple, and/or a National DMDA support group, can focus on specific ways to restore and strengthen the intimacy
- Certain antidepressant medications may hamper sexual functioning, leading to greater difficulties between partners. Speak with your doctor or mental health professional about options

My husband has been treated with antidepressant medications for over three years. Recently, I was also diagnosed with depression. It took him almost two years to find a medication that does not affect our personal life. I am scared of the same thing happening with me. How can I avoid this? Are there any questions I should ask my doctor to avoid the same problem?

I assume you are referring to the sexual side effects of some antidepressants. Some of the newer medications have a much lower incidence of such side effects. Talk to your doctor about your options. Whichever antidepressant he or she decides to start you on, be sure to ask about all of its potential side effects. If side effects develop, discuss them with your doctor and decide whether the problem is severe enough for you to switch medications.

—DR. ROBERT HIRSCHFELD

WHEN THERE ARE CHILDREN AT HOME

I have been taking an antidepressant medication because I was unable to get out of bed or go to work. Interaction with my family was difficult and my children started asking my husband "What is wrong with mommy?" First, how do I explain this to them? Second, how do I explain why I am taking medication, as they see me taking it every morning?

It depends on how old your children are, of course, but based on what you think they can understand I'd suggest starting by saying, "Mom hasn't been feeling well and she's taking some medication that will make her better." If your kids are teenagers, you can say that "Mom has depression and is taking a medication to help her with this illness."

Children may not be able to express their concerns, especially if the treatment goes on for a long time, but they may be fearful. In some cases, family therapy may be helpful.

—DR. DAVID DUNNER

What's a good way to begin talking to my children about my illness? In particular, a teenager who wants to pretend that nothing is wrong, and who begins to resent or ignore the parent who has depression?

All children want to know what's to become of *them* when something difficult is going on in their family. They will see your depression, like everything, in terms of how it affects them. When I was at a low, almost suicidal, I remember my preteen daughter saying, "But you told me you'd take me to the mall!" She saw me crying a lot, and when she asked I'd just say that I didn't know what was wrong. There were moments when I just had to get up from the dinner table because I couldn't deal with it. When I was feeling better I'd tell her I was going through something hard. If I told her I was depressed, she just thought that meant I was sad. She knew when I had my doctor appointments and that I was taking medication, but she didn't want a lot of detail. She just wanted to know that I was going to be okay.

Explain to your teenagers how their lives may be interrupted, who will take care of them, what there will be to hold on to. Get help from others to minimize the disruption to your children's lives. Most important, make sure they understand that it's not their fault.

They may want to know about your treatment. Explain that it's going to help you but that it will take time. Naturally you must first take into account your children's developmental level in figuring out how to explain your illness. Adolescents may also be concerned about their chances of inheriting depression. It may be comforting for you, as an adult, to know the disorder didn't come out of the blue, that it clusters in families, but for an adolescent it's not comforting at all to know they are at risk of suffering from depression too. So, even hard information—like the fact that there's a four times greater chance of having depressive episodes if someone in the family has them—will have a different effect on children.

Your children need a conflict-free zone where everything stays the same, whether that's school, sports, or friends. The teenager who resents or ignores you could be doing that for a hundred reasons. The parent who recognizes the ambivalence will be better able to deal with it. Family counseling might be wise to consider, either for crisis management or more long-term help. Family therapy can be most important following a family member's depression, when the person is feeling well enough to make use of it. That's the time to make a plan and to educate the rest of the family about depression. They can learn specific problem-solving skills and air their concerns, fears, and anger. Sometimes guidance counselors at school can be outlets for children's feelings.

—DR. MARTHA MANNING

Are children of a depressed parent more likely than other children to develop problems in school, behavioral problems, or depression itself?

Yes, yes, and yes. A depressed mother or father will be less able to give of themselves or to function in a normal way. Children in such homes will feel the negative consequences. And since we know that there are genetic factors, these children also face the possibility of inheriting the disease. If they become depressed as children, then they may be more likely to have problems concentrating, they may be less motivated, they may have less energy, and they may be irritable and socially withdrawn. All these factors can lead to school and behavioral problems.

As a parent, you should be on the lookout for signs of depression in your child and get it treated quickly. The signs of depression would be the same as in an adult: loss of energy, difficulty concentrating, sleeping too much or too little, eating too much or too little, and loss of interest in things they used to enjoy.

—DR. ROBERT HIRSCHFELD

CHAPTER 4

GETTING THE HELP
YOU NEED

FINDING THE DOCTOR YOU NEED

When I am looking for a doctor, what kind of questions should I ask to determine if he or she understands depression and its treatments?

Here are a few questions to start. What percentage of your practice deals with patients with mood disorders? What's your general approach to treatment—are you likely to recommend psychotherapy or medication? How do you integrate family members and friends into treatment? How accessible are you? How often are you on call? What would the goals of my treatment be? Don't forget to ask about insurance coverage and whether doctor's fees can be offered on a sliding scale.

Most important is your sense of being able to talk with the doctor. Some doctors won't even answer such questions, which tells you a lot.

—DR. MARTHA MANNING

I was diagnosed with depression by my primary care doctor. Do I need to see a psychiatrist also?

Not necessarily. Primary care practitioners write more than half the prescriptions for antidepressants. Many of these doctors do an outstanding job of treating their patients and keeping track of the effects of their medication. If you have a good relationship with your doctor, you don't necessarily need a psychiatrist.

The exceptions would be if you have manic-depressive illness (bipolar disorder), if you haven't responded well after your doctor has tried two antidepressant medications, if your depression is so severe that you require hospitalization, if you're so incapacitated that you're unable to get out of bed in the morning or go to work, or if you feel suicidal.

—DR. ROBERT HIRSCHFELD

If your physician seems knowledgeable and you have a trusting relationship and open communication with him or her, discuss the question of whether seeing a psychiatrist would be appropriate. While it could be helpful, it might not be necessary.

—DR. DREW PINSKY

My primary care doctor, who prescribed my antidepressants, never mentioned that it was possible for the medications to affect me sexually, but a friend who is taking the same medication told me this was possible. Should I find a new doctor? A psychiatrist? If my doctor doesn't know that this is a problem should I look for someone who does? Is there a reason why he never told me about this possible problem?

Doctors don't always mention *all* the possible side effects when you're starting out, because many of them are unlikely to show up. The most common ones should be mentioned to you, though. Aside from sexual problems, these include, for the tricyclics: sleepiness, dry mouth, and dizziness; for the SSRIs: nausea, agitation, and insomnia; and for some of the newer medications: nausea, agitation, dizziness, and insomnia.

You should give your doctor a chance to discuss this situation with you before considering any change in health care provider. I think it's a mistake not to discuss it with the person who's prescribing the medication. If you continue to feel that you are not getting all the information you want, you may then consider changing to another doctor. It is important for you to be comfortable with your health care professional.

—DR. DAVID DUNNER

Some doctors are really not aware of how distressing and common the sexual side effects from antidepressant medication can be. The physician may be well trained and have had significant experience prescribing antidepressant medication. However, it may be that he or she is focusing on the primary symptoms of depression, rather than some of the elements that hinder a thorough and complete recovery, such as side effects from the medications.

I would recommend that before you decide to find a new doctor, you try communicating clearly and effectively with the one you have.

Here are some questions for you to consider as you decide whether you want to stay with your current doctor: Is your illness being followed closely by your doctor? Have your symptoms lessened or disappeared? Are you experiencing any side effects? Have you reported side effects to your doctor? Are you comfortable discussing very personal issues, such as sexual dysfunction, with your doctor? Is your doctor open to discussing the side effects with you when you have raised this topic, and does he or she seem knowledgeable about them? Is your doctor communicating with you about other important issues, such as the possible need for individual and/or couples psychotherapy or the estimated duration of antidepressant treatment?

—DR. DREW PINSKY

I've been taking an antidepressant for several months and think it has caused sexual problems. How do I talk to my doctor? He always seems to be in such a rush.

Get clear on what you want to say. Be specific about what kind of sexual problems you're experiencing. Is it different from any problem you might have had from the depression itself? Are you having trouble getting aroused, staying aroused, achieving orgasm? Do you have a general feeling of being "dead" sexually?

Understand that you deserve to have this issue taken seriously. You deserve to get "back to normal" as much as you can, as quickly as possible. Write down your concerns so you don't forget what you

WHEN VISITING THE DOCTOR

- Set appointment goals
- Prepare notes or a checklist ahead of time
- Write down anything complicated the doctor tells you
- If you have specific concerns to discuss, ask for an appointment when the doctor is less rushed
- If you will feel more comfortable, ask for the first part of the exam to take place in the doctor's office rather than the exam room
- Make follow-up appointments to discuss treatment and side effects

want to say. Schedule the first or last appointment of the day, or the first appointment after lunch, so the doctor will be in less of a hurry. If you feel ridiculous in that paper gown, tell the receptionist when you make the appointment to schedule some extra time for a consultation—in the doctor's office. If you become embarrassed when the receptionist asks why, say you'd like to keep it to yourself or that it's about side effects from the treatment. Or ask to speak with a nurse practitioner or the physician assistant at the office, who might be more available to speak with you at length. Consider writing down your concerns and mailing or e-mailing them ahead of time. If you find your doctor is not taking you seriously or not giving you enough time, it might be time to find a new one.

—DR. MARTHA MANNING

I am not feeling "sexual" lately and I am not sure why. I am embarrassed to speak about it with my doctor, but I am getting married soon, and would like to be able to enjoy those feelings again. Are there ways that I can make this awkward conversation easier?

> ### DEPRESSION ISSUES TO DISCUSS WITH YOUR DOCTOR
>
> - Medication dosage and timing
> - Possible side effects
> - Switching or changing medication if treatment is not working
> - Behavior modification (such as reducing alcohol intake)
> - Best way to reach your doctor if you experience a severe side effect
> - Length of time before you feel better
> - Psychotherapy options
> - Local support groups
> - Where to find additional information

If you suspect your lack of sexual feeling is from an antidepressant medication, how is it different from problems you may have had before? Is it because of the depression itself? Marriage is a major life change. Try to clarify your thoughts as much as you can. It may not be an easy conversation with your doctor, but you must bring yourself to do it. If it makes it easier, provide your questions to the doctor ahead of time.

Talk to your fiancé about it, too. Bring him with you to the appointment. This is something you'll have to deal with together over time, regardless of the cause.

—DR. MARTHA MANNING

PROBLEMS WITH INSURANCE COVERAGE

I am seeing a therapist for my depression, but I can only see her three or four times a year because beyond that my insurance stops paying for it. What can I do?

Mental health coverage has always been more restrictive than coverage for other medical treatment, and with the changes in health care management it's become even more difficult to afford good mental health care. You do have some options, though.

Explain your problem to your therapist and ask her whether she would consider lowering her fee. You might be able to continue seeing her and pay out-of-pocket. Some therapists are willing to see patients at less busy times—like the middle of the day—for a reduced fee. Also ask her whether she might go to bat for you with the insurance company. She might not win, but it's worth a try.

Another possibility would be switching to a more affordable therapist. The fees vary greatly. Psychiatrists typically charge between $150 and $200 an hour. Social workers charge about half that, and psychologists fall somewhere in between. You should also look into clinics that charge on a sliding scale, basing their charges on what you can afford.

If you can't arrange for more than three or four visits a year with your therapist, spread them out and use them to focus on coping strategies that you can practice between sessions.

You can also take advantage of low-cost or no-cost support groups through organizations like National DMDA. There are National DMDA support groups across the United States. Hearing other people's stories and how they manage their depression may help you tremendously and give you a ready-made support network in addition to your therapy. But remember, support groups are no substitute for professional care.

—DR. LAURA EPSTEIN ROSEN

My insurance company apparently covers only certain antidepressant medications and my doctor wants me to take one that is not covered. I'm not sure that I can afford this out of my own pocket. What can I do?

In a shortsighted effort to cut pharmacy costs, many insurance plans have limited access to some medications. The newer antidepressants are more expensive than the old ones, and therefore sometimes are not covered—even though your overall medical bills may be higher if you're not getting the medication that's best for you.

What to do? Go with what's covered (if this is your first treatment); then work with your doctor to petition the insurance company to allow the prescription your doctor wants. If a good rationale is provided (such as you haven't responded to the drug they cover), you may be surprised to find that they will make an exception.

Your alternatives would be to pay for the preferred drug yourself (most antidepressants cost about $2 a day) or to see if the pharmaceutical company that manufactures it can provide samples or special plans to make it available to you if you are legitimately unable to pay for it. Many pharmaceutical companies offer patient assistance programs to provide prescription medicines free of cost to physicians whose patients might not otherwise have access to necessary medicines. For more information, have your doctor contact the company directly. If you do not know who manufactures a certain medication, ask your pharmacist or doctor.

—Dr. David Dunner

CHAPTER 5

RESOURCES

SELF TESTS

SYMPTOMS OF DEPRESSIVE DISORDERS

Anyone experiencing four or more of the following symptoms of depression and/or mania should seek help from a medical professional if symptoms persist for longer than two weeks.

Symptoms of Depression

- Prolonged sadness or unexplained crying spells
- Significant changes in appetite, sleep patterns
- Irritability, anger, worry, agitation, anxiety
- Pessimism, indifference
- Loss of energy, persistent tiredness
- Feelings of guilt, worthlessness
- Inability to concentrate, indecisiveness
- Inability to take pleasure in former interests, social withdrawal
- Unexplained aches and pains
- Recurring thoughts of death or suicide

If you have recurring thoughts of death or suicide, contact a mental health professional, clergy member, family member, or friend *immediately!*

Manic depression (bipolar disorder) differs significantly from clinical depression. In manic-depressive illness, a person's mood alternates between mania and depression. The mood swing can last for days, weeks, or even months. It is important to inform your mental health professional of *all* mood swings, past or present. Treatments for depression and manic depression are different and a correct diagnosis is important.

Symptoms of Mania

- Heightened mood, exaggerated optimism and self-confidence

- Decreased need for sleep without fatigue

- Grandiose delusions, inflated sense of self-importance

- Excessive irritability, aggressive behavior

- Increased physical, mental activity

- Racing speech, flight of ideas, impulsiveness

- Poor judgement, easily distracted

- Reckless behavior such as spending sprees, rash business decisions, erratic driving, sexual indiscretions

- In most severe cases, auditory hallucinations (hearing voices)

HOW MUCH TROUBLE HAS YOUR PARTNER'S DEPRESSION CAUSED YOU AND YOUR RELATIONSHIP?

Answer each question by circling "Yes" or "No."

1. Yes No   Do you feel less attractive or unsure of yourself sexually because he/she has been less interested in having sex with you?

2. Yes No   Are the two of you having other sexual problems?

3. Yes No   Are you less interested in spending time with him/her?

4. Yes No   Do you feel frustrated because you are pushed away when you attempt to help?

5. Yes No   Do you find yourself spending so much time with your partner that you no longer have time for other people and activities?

6. Yes No   Are you experiencing any signs of depression yourself, such as feeling down, being less interested in your usual activities, taking less pleasure in life, having trouble with sleep, weight, appetite, concentration, energy level, and/or feelings of worthlessness?

7. Yes No   Are you and your partner arguing more intensely and/or more often?

8. Yes No   Are you "picking up the slack" so much that you feel overburdened?

9. Yes No   Are you feeling more stress at work or school?

10. Yes No   Are you feeling more isolated and lonely than usual?

11. Yes No   Do you feel more tense and anxious?

12. Yes No   Have you and your partner been considering a separation or divorce?

13. Yes No Have you and/or your partner been drinking more than usual or using unprescribed drugs?

14. Yes No Have you or your partner lost income, due either to job loss or missed work, since the depression started?

15. Yes No Do you worry a lot of the time that your partner no longer has the will to live?

16. Yes No Are the two of you having communication problems such as frequently interrupting each other, putting each other down, and/or not listening to one another?

17. Yes No Are you and your partner more competitive with each other than usual?

18. Yes No Are you having more physical problems than usual, such as unexplained aches and pains?

SCORING

Count the number of times you circled "YES" to get your "Trouble with Depression" score.

Severe Trouble: Time to seek help

18 to 13 You and your relationship are definitely affected by your partner's depression. You are experiencing many of the classic secondary effects of depression and are at risk for depression yourself. Your relationship is also suffering significantly from your partner's depression and the negative interactions between the two of you will likely result in a worsening of his/her depression. Your relationship may be at risk for severe problems such as communication breakdowns, separation, or even divorce. You and your loved one should definitely gather more information on depression's effects on loved ones and relationships. You should also consult with a mental health professional for both yourself and your relationship.

Moderate Trouble: Time to be concerned

12 to 7   You and your relationship are affected by your partner's depression. You may be feeling overburdened, resentful, stressed, and/or distant from your partner. The two of you may be arguing more frequently and intensely. You should gather more information about depression and its secondary effects. You may also want to consult with a mental health professional for the sake of both yourself and your relationship. If you act now you can neutralize depression's toxic effects on you and your relationship before your reach the Severe Trouble stage.

Little or No Trouble: Keep your eyes open

6 or less Although you and your relationship may be experiencing some difficulties, depression is no more likely than other factors to have caused the trouble. However, because depression is so common and its effects on loved ones and relationships can be negative, it is always a good idea to keep your eyes open to the warning signs described in this questionnaire.

Source: Laura Epstein Rosen, Ph.D. and Xavier Francisco Amador, Ph.D., *When Someone You Love Is Depressed,* New York: Fireside, 1996, 60-61.

GUIDED QUESTIONNAIRES
FOR MEN AND WOMEN

Many people experiencing depression notice a decrease in sexual desire and may have fewer thoughts about any type of sexual activity. At times this decrease in desire is part of the depression, and when the depression begins to lift, the sexual feelings return. At other times, decreased sexual desire develops as a result of tension or dissatisfaction in a couple's relationship. Sexual problems associated with stress or relationship issues will often improve if the partners make an effort to improve the overall quality of their relationship.

Sometimes, however, the sexual problems may be related to antidepressant medication prescribed to treat the depression. The following questions are designed to help determine if the medication may be causing the sexual problems.

If a change in sexual functioning occurs within a few weeks of starting a new antidepressant, the next step would be to speak with your healthcare professional, who would then work with you to resolve the problem. Because depression is a serious medical illness, it is important not to suddenly stop taking the prescribed medication without first consulting your physician.

If you and your partner are getting along well and do not think the decrease in sexual interest is due to a relationship problem, then the following questions may help determine if the sexual problem is related to the medication being taken. Talk with your doctor if you answer "yes" to any of the following questions. Please note that the sexual behaviors listed here fall within the range of normal sexual activity for adults; however, not all types of sexual activities are universally practiced or appealing to every person.

GUIDED QUESTIONNAIRE FOR MEN

1. Have you noticed a change in sexual activities or function (for example sexual urge, drive, or ability to get and/or maintain an erection, reach orgasm and/or ejaculate)?

   If you noticed a change, did it begin

   - before you became depressed?
   - around the same time you became aware of your depression?
   - a few weeks after you started taking your antidepressant medication?

Sexual Desire/Sex Drive

2. Independent of your partner's sexual drive, has there been a change in your libido, sexual desire/sex drive?

3. Has there been a change in frequency of intercourse?

4. Has there been a change in frequency of sexual thoughts or fantasies?

5. Has there been a change in the frequency of masturbation?

Arousal

6. Has there been a change in your ability to get an erection sufficient for penetration with some manual assistance?

7. Are you having problems getting and maintaining erections with your partner?

8. Are you having problems getting an erection with manual stimulation or masturbation?

9. Have you experienced a decrease in the number of mornings you awake with a firm penis?

10. Are the erections you currently experience sufficient for penetration if intercourse were to occur?

Orgasm

11. Has there been a change in your ability to experience orgasm or climax?

12. Has there been a change in your ability to ejaculate?

Additional Information

13. Could these changes be related to
    - relationship problems (arguments, a change in feelings toward your partner)?
    - a change in your personal situation (illness in partner/family member, financial problems, stress, etc.)?

GUIDED QUESTIONNAIRE FOR WOMEN

1. Have you noticed a change in sexual activities or function (for example sexual urge, drive, or ability to reach orgasm)?

   If you noticed a change, did it begin

   - before you became depressed?
   - around the same time you became aware of your depression?
   - a few weeks after you started taking your medication for depression?

Sexual Desire/Sex Drive

2. Independent of your partner's sexual needs, has there been a change in your sexual desire/sex drive or urge to engage in any type of sexual activity?

3. Has there been a change in frequency of intercourse?

4. Has there been a change in how often you initiate sexual activity?

5. Has there been a change in frequency of sexual thoughts or fantasies?

6. Has there been a change in the frequency of masturbation?

Arousal

7. Has there been a change in your ability to get sexually aroused or excited? Does this occur under all situations with your partner and in masturbation? Has there been a change in lubrication (wetness) during sexual activity?

8. Has there been a change in your use of over-the-counter vaginal lubricants?

9. Are you experiencing pain during sexual activity?

Orgasm

10. Has there been a change in how long it takes you to climax or reach orgasm?

11. Has there been a change in your ability to experience orgasm?

Additional Information

13. Could these changes be related to

- relationship problems (arguments, a change in feelings toward your partner)?

- a change in your personal situation (illness in partner/family member, financial problems, stress, etc.)?

Guided Questionnaire for Men and Guided Questionnaire for Women created in consultation with Kathleen Segraves, Ph.D. and R. Taylor Segraves, M.D., Ph.D.

WHERE TO GO
FOR ADDITIONAL
INFORMATION
OR HELP

MENTAL HEALTH ORGANIZATIONS

American Academy of Child and Adolescent Psychiatry (AACAP)
3615 Wisconsin Ave., NW
Washington, DC 20016
Telephone: (202) 966-7300
Web site: www.aacap.org

The American Academy of Child and Adolescent Psychiatry (AACAP) is dedicated to treating and improving the quality of life for children, adolescents, and families affected by mental, behavioral, or developmental disorders.

AACAP offers information on child and adolescent psychiatry, fact sheets for parents and caregivers, current research, practice guidelines, managed care information, awards and fellowship descriptions, meeting information, and more.

American Association for Geriatric Psychiatry (AAGP)
7910 Woodmont Ave., Suite 1050
Bethesda, MD 20815
Telephone: (301) 654-7850
Web site: www.aagpgpa.org

The American Association for Geriatric Psychiatry (AAGP) is a national association dedicated to promoting the mental health and well-being of older people and improving the care of those with late-life mental disorders.

AAGP enhances the knowledge base and standards of practice in geriatric psychiatry through education and research, and by advocating for the mental health needs of older Americans. For consumers, the Association offers free information including brochures, geriatric psychiatry referrals, and answers to 10 key questions about HMOs and mental health services.

American Association for Marriage and Family Therapy (AAMFT)
1133 15th St., NW, Suite 300
Washington, DC 20005
Telephone: (202) 452-0109
Web site: www.aamft.org

The American Association for Marriage and Family Therapy (AAMFT) works to increase understanding, research, and education in the field of marriage and family therapy, and ensure that the public's needs are met by trained practitioners.

AAMFT publishes the *Journal of Marital and Family Therapy* and *Family Therapy News*, and a variety of brochures and pamphlets that inform the public about the field of marriage and family therapy.

Anxiety Disorders Association of America (ADAA)
11900 Parklawn Dr., Suite 100
Rockville, MD 20852
Telephone: (301) 231-9350
Web site: www.adaa.org

The Anxiety Disorders Association of America (ADAA) promotes the prevention and cure of anxiety disorders and works to improve the lives of all people who suffer from them. The Association is made up of professionals who conduct research and treat anxiety disorders and individuals who have a personal or general interest in learning more about such disorders.

ADAA offers numerous educational materials, including pamphlets, self-help books, audio tapes, and a newsletter for professionals and consumers.

American Psychiatric Association (APA)
1400 K St., NW
Washington, DC 20005
Telephone: (202) 682-6000
Web site: www.psych.org

The American Psychiatric Association (APA) seeks to further the study of the nature, treatment, and prevention of mental disorders.

Although APA's core audience is professionals, the organization offers a wide range of resources to consumers, including fact sheets on a variety of mental health problems, videos on mental illness, APA library and publications, a pamphlet series, and a suggested reading list. Many of these materials are available in Spanish. In addition, APA provides hotline numbers and the phone numbers of other organizations that can help.

American Psychological Association (APA)
750 First St., NE
Washington, DC 20002-4242
Telephone: (202) 336-5700/(800) 374-3120
Web site: www.apa.org

The American Psychological Association (APA) works to advance psychology as a science, a profession, and a means of promoting human welfare.

Primarily a professional organization, APA has several resources that provide information on mental health and psychological issues to consumers. Resources include brochures addressing relevant topics, such as women and depression, talking to someone who can help with depression, and recovering from depression. There is a help center on APA's web site, and other useful information is available by calling its toll-free number.

Bazelon Center
1101 15th St. NW, Suite 1212
Washington, DC 20005
Telephone: (212) 467-5730
Web site: www.bazelon.org

The Bazelon Center utilizes litigation and policy reform to uphold the legal rights of people with mental disabilities. Among other services, the Center offers consumer publications and advocacy manuals.

Depression After Delivery

P.O. Box 1282
Morrisville, PA 19607
Telephone: (800) 944-4773
Web site: www. infotrail.com/dad/dad.html

Depression After Delivery is a national self-help organization providing support, education, information, and referrals for women coping with the blues, anxiety, depression, and psychosis associated with the arrival of a baby.

With more than 100 affiliated groups nationwide, Depression After Delivery provides information on postpartum depression and maintains an intensive effort to eliminate the stigma attached to the disorder. In addition to several information packages, it offers a reader-friendly newsletter.

National Alliance for the Mentally Ill (NAMI)

200 North Glebe Rd., Suite 1015
Arlington, VA 22203-3754
Help line: (800) 950-NAMI
Web site: www.nami.org

The National Alliance for the Mentally Ill (NAMI) was founded by families of mentally ill people who were frustrated by the lack of reliable resources. The organization's objectives include providing emotional support and practical guidance for families, and educating and informing the public about mental illness.

NAMI offers valuable educational resources including brochures, newsletters, information on local support groups, books, and videos. In addition, NAMI's help line provides information about mental illness and the phone numbers of local and state NAMI affiliates.

National Association of Social Workers (NASW)
750 First St., NE, Suite 700
Washington, DC 20002-4241
Telephone: (800) 638-8799
Web site: www.socialworkers.org

The National Association of Social Workers (NASW) is the largest professional association of social workers, with over 155,000 members worldwide. There are Chapter offices in each of the 50 states as well as Puerto Rico and the Virgin Islands. NASW has a Clinical Register that lists licensed clinical social workers who practice as mental health professionals. NASW is a partner with the Campaign on Clinical Depression and participates in year-round depression screenings throughouut the country to encourage consumers to seek diagnosis and treatment.

National Depressive and Manic-Depressive Association (National DMDA)
730 North Franklin St., Suite 501
Chicago, IL 60610-3526
Telephone: (800) 826-3632
Depression Screening Site Information: (888) 424-4410
Web site: www.ndmda.org

The National Depressive and Manic-Depressive Association (National DMDA) is the largest patient-run, illness-specific organization in the country. Through its global network of nearly 300 active chapters and support groups, National DMDA works to educate the public and health care community about the nature and management of depressive and manic-depressive illnesses as treatable medical diseases, to improve access to care, and to advocate for research toward the elimination of these illnesses.

Services available to consumers include videotapes and publications on depressive disorders (including Spanish-language brochures), a bookstore with more than 70 titles of printed and audiovisual materials about various types of depressive illnesses, consumer conferences, and contact information for local support groups.

National Foundation for Depressive Illness (NAFDI)
P.O. Box 2257
New York, NY 10116
Telephone: (800) 239-1265
Web site: www.depression.org

The National Foundation for Depressive Illness (NAFDI) is a non-profit organization whose goal is to increase public awareness about depression. NAFDI provides much-needed information about the consequences and treatment of depression.

Through the NAFDI help line, the organization offers information about symptoms of depression, as well as referral lists of local support groups and doctors who specialize in treating depression. In addition, it provides information on useful articles, magazines, and books.

National Institute of Mental Health (NIMH)
6001 Executive Blvd.
Bethesda, MD 20892
Telephone: (800) 421-4211
Web site: www.nimh.nih.gov

The National Institute of Mental Health (NIMH) works to increase public recognition of the symptoms of depression and knowledge of how and where to get a professional diagnosis and treatment.

The NIMH web site offers information to consumers about depression through brochures, information sheets, reports, press releases, fact sheets, and other educational materials. Many of these materials are also available in Spanish. NIMH encourages people to call their toll-free number for a brochure on depression, or visit their Web site for quick access to a fact sheet.

National Mental Health Association (NMHA)
1021 Prince St.
Alexandria, VA 22314
Information line: (800) 969-NMHA
For free brochures: (800) 228-1114
Web site: www.nmha.org

The National Mental Health Association (NMHA) is dedicated to promoting mental health, preventing mental disorders, and achieving victory over mental illnesses through advocacy, education, research, and service. Its information line and web site offer numerous useful educational materials and brochures on depression in both English and Spanish.

National Mental Illness Screening Project (NMISP)

One Washington St., Suite 304
Wellesley Hills, MA 02481-1706
Phone: (781) 239-0071
Web site: www.nmisp.org

The National Mental Illness Screening Project (NMISP) is a nonprofit organization developed to coordinate nationwide mental health screening programs and to ensure cooperation, professionalism, and accountability in mental illness screenings.

Programs implemented by NMISP, all of which are offered to the public free of charge, include National Depression Screening Day and an interactive telephone screening program. National Depression Screening Day, a community-based initiative, is conducted by local health professionals with materials provided by NMISP.

Obsessive-Compulsive Foundation

9 Depot St.
Milford, CT 06460
Telephone: (203) 878-5669
Web site: www.ocfoundation.org

The Foundation provides support and information to patients with obsessive-compulsive disorder, as well as their families. It provides a newsletter, brochures, and anxiety disorders screenings.

SUICIDE PREVENTION ORGANIZATIONS

American Foundation for Suicide Prevention (AFSP)
120 Wall St., Fl. 22
New York, NY 10005
Telephone: (888) 333-2377/(212) 363-3500
National Suicide Hotline: (800) 999-9999
Web site: www.afsp.org

The American Foundation for Suicide Prevention (AFSP) is dedicated to the advancement of knowledge about suicide and its prevention.

AFSP supports research projects that help further the understanding and treatment of depression and suicide. AFSP advocates suicide-prevention education and holds conferences, takes part in training, publishes a newsletter, and provides informational literature. AFSP also has organized a national directory of support groups.

American Association of Suicidology (AAS)
4201 Connecticut Ave., NW, Suite 408
Washington, DC 20008
Telephone: (202) 237-2280
Web site: www.suicidology.org

The American Association of Suicidology (AAS) is dedicated to the understanding and prevention of suicide. AAS promotes research, public awareness programs, and education and training for professionals and volunteers.

The organization offers educational materials and refers people to suicide hotlines and support groups. In addition, it provides services for people who have survived a suicide including support groups, newsletters, and conferences. AAS also provides a wide range of resources that includes books on suicide prevention, newsletters, pamphlets, school guidelines, support group guidelines, and a support group directory.

Suicide Prevention Advocacy Network (SPAN)
5034 Odin's Way
Marietta, GA 30068
Telephone: (770) 998-8819
Web site: www.spanusa.org

The Suicide Prevention Advocacy Network (SPAN) is a nonprofit organization dedicated to the creation of an effective national suicide prevention strategy. The organization links the energy of those bereaved by suicide with the expertise of leaders in science, business, government, and public service to achieve the goal of significantly reducing the national rate of suicide by the year 2010. SPAN offers a newsletter, facts about suicide, and advocacy information.

OTHER USEFUL ORGANIZATIONS

Men's Health Network (MHN)
P.O. Box 75972
Washington, DC 20013
Hotline: (888) MEN-2-MEN
Web site: www.info@menshealthnetwork.org

A nonprofit, charitable corporation, the Men's Health Network (MHN) works to promote public and media awareness of men's health issues and to disseminate vital information on how to prevent disease, violence, and addiction.

MHN is currently developing a data collection system to act as a national clearinghouse for information about men's health issues. MHN also provides and maintains an ongoing network of health care providers and services that deal with men's health issues.

National Women's Health Resource Center (NWHRC)
120 Albany St., Suite 820
New Brunswick, NJ 08901
Telephone: (877) 986-9472/(732) 828-8575
Web site: www.healthywomen.org

The National Women's Health Resource Center, Inc. (NWHRC) is a national clearinghouse for women's health information. NWHRC's *National Women's Health Report* provides comprehensive, unbiased information on health. It is recognized by consumers, health care providers, and professional organizations for its ability to translate often confusing and technical medical information and scientific research into terms that are easier to understand.

NWHRC also offers a bimonthly newsletter, which often covers topics related to depression. Consumers can call the hotline and/or main number for more information or to receive educational materials.

Sexual Function Health Council
American Foundation for Urologic Disease (AFUD)
300 West Pratt St., Suite 401
Baltimore, MD 21201
Telephone: (800) 242-2383
Web site: www.afud.org

The mission of the American Foundation for Urologic Disease (AFUD) is the prevention and cure of urologic disease. To this end, AFUD handles up to 5,000 calls each month on its toll-free information lines. Under the auspices of the AFUD, more than $2.4 million is earmarked for research and public education initiatives, and over six million brochures have been distributed to patients nationwide. AFUD publishes *Family Urology,* the official magazine of the Foundation.

RECOMMENDED READING

PERSONAL STORIES

Call Me Anna: The Autobiography of Patty Duke by Patty Duke

Darkness Visible: A Memoir of Madness by William Styron

Undercurrents: A Life Beneath the Surface by Martha Manning, Ph.D.

An Unquiet Mind: A Memoir of Moods and Madness by Kay Redfield Jamison, Ph.D.

Willow Weep for Me, A Black Woman's Journey through Depression: A Memoir by Meri Nana-Anna Danquah

The Beast: A Journey through Depression by Tracy Thompson

READING FOR PARTNERS AND FAMILIES

Helping Someone with Mental Illness: A Compassionate Guide for Family, Friends and Caregivers by Rosalyn Carter

When Someone You Love Is Depressed: How to Help Your Loved One without Losing Yourself by Laura Epstein Rosen, Ph.D., and Xavier Francisco Amador, Ph.D.

How You Can Survive When They're Depressed: Living and Coping with Depression Fallout by Anne Sheffield

GENERAL REFERENCE

The Depression Workbook: A Guide for Living with Depression and Manic Depression by Mary Ellen Copeland, M.A., M.S.

A Mood Apart: Depression, Mania and Other Afflictions of the Self by Peter C. Whybrow, M.D.

MEDICATIONS CURRENTLY PRESCRIBED TO TREAT DEPRESSION

Medication Class	Medication Trade Names	Mechanism of Action in the Brain	Possible Side Effects
MAOI			
Monoamine Oxidase Inhibitor	Nardil® Parnate®	+Serotonin +Norepinephrine +Dopamine	Fatal interactions with other antidepressants Dizziness Interaction with some foods
MOOD STABILIZER			
(Antidepressant augmentation)	Eskalith® Lithobid® Lithonate®	+Serotonin	Tremor High overdose toxicity Dry mouth
NDRI			
Norepinephrine Dopamine Reuptake Inhibitor	Wellbutrin SR®	+Norepinephrine +Dopamine	Agitation Insomnia Anxiety
SSNRI			
Selective Serotonin Norepinephrine Reuptake Inhibitor	Effexor® Effexor XR®	+Serotonin +Norepinephrine	Agitation Nausea Dizziness Sleepiness Sexual dysfunction

Medication Class	Medication Trade Names	Mechanism of Action in the Brain	Possible Side Effects
SSRI			
Selective Serotonin Reuptake Inhibitor	Celexa® Luvox® Paxil® Prozac® Zoloft®	+Serotonin	Nausea Insomnia Sleepiness Agitation Sexual dysfunction
SSRIB			
Selective Serotonin Reuptake Inhibitor and Blocker	Deseryl® Serzone®	+Serotonin	Nausea Dizziness Sleepiness
TCA			
Tricyclic Antidepressant	Anafranil® Elavil® Norpramin® Pamelor® Surmontil® Tofranil® Vivactil®	+Serotonin +Norepinephrine (Depending on medication)	Sleepiness Nervousness Dizziness Dry mouth Constipation High overdose toxicity
TETRACYCLIC			
	Remeron®	+Serotonin +Norepinephrine	Sleepiness Weight gain Dizziness

CONTRIBUTOR
BIOGRAPHIES

ANITA H. CLAYTON, M.D.

Anita H. Clayton, M.D. is an Associate Professor and Vice-Chair, Department of Psychiatric Medicine at the University of Virginia Health System in Charlottesville. Dr. Clayton also holds the positions of Medical Director for the Center for Psychiatric Clinical Research and Director of Psychiatric Ambulatory Services at the same institution.

Dr. Clayton's areas of expertise include sexual dysfunction and mood disorders associated with reproductive life events in women. Her research has been published in several journals and she is a regular speaker on sexual dysfunction related to depression at medical grand rounds and conferences. Dr. Clayton also speaks about depression and its treatment at local seminars and fairs, and has been involved in activities and programs for the National Depression Screening Day since 1992.

Dr. Clayton earned her medical degree and completed her undergraduate work at the University of Virginia. She also completed her internship and residency at the University of Virginia Hospital in the Department of Behavioral Medicine and Psychiatry. She is board certified by the American Board of Psychiatry and Neurology and is a fellow in the American Psychiatric Association.

DAVID L. DUNNER, M.D.

David L. Dunner, M.D. is a professor in the Department of Psychiatry and Behavioral Sciences and Director of the Center for Anxiety and Depression at the University of Washington in Seattle.

Dr. Dunner's areas of research include mood and anxiety disorders, with a special focus on psychopharmacological treatment of these conditions, and clinical description of bipolar and unipolar affective disorders.

Dr. Dunner has authored or coauthored more than 200 publications, and was the editor for the recent textbook *Current Psychiatric Therapy II* (W.B. Saunders Company, 1997). He serves on the editorial board of several scientific journals and is the editor-in-chief of *Comprehensive Psychiatry* and the co-editor of *The Psychiatric Clinics of North America: Annual of Drug Therapy.*

Trained at the Washington University School of Medicine, Dr. Dunner spent two years at the National Institute of Mental Health, involved in research studies in bipolar depression. He serves on the Scientific Advisory Board of the National Depressive and Manic-Depressive Association (National DMDA). Dr. Dunner is a regularly invited speaker for local chapters of National DMDA and NAMI.

ROBERT M.A. HIRSCHFELD, M.D.

Robert M.A. Hirschfeld, M.D., is the Titus H. Harris Distinguished Professor and Chair of the Department of Psychiatry and Behavioral Sciences at the University of Texas Medical Branch at Galveston.

Dr. Hirschfeld is one of the nation's leading advocates for the mentally ill, and is on the Scientific Advisory Board of National DMDA. Dr. Hirschfeld is known internationally for his research in the diagnosis and treatment of depression and anxiety and has made major contributions to the understanding of the classification of depression.

The author of more than 200 scientific papers and abstracts, Dr. Hirschfeld has received numerous honors, including the Jan Fawcett Humanitarian Award from National DMDA. He is also listed in *The Best Doctors in America, 1998–1999.*

Dr. Hirschfeld received his medical degree from the University of Michigan in 1968. He received an M.S. in Operations Research from Stanford University in 1972, where he completed his residency in psychiatry that same year. The American Board of Psychiatry and Neurology certified Dr. Hirschfeld in 1975.

MARTHA M. MANNING, PH.D.

Martha Manning, Ph.D. is a writer and clinical psychologist from Arlington,Virginia, and former professor of psychology at George Mason University. She is the author of three books including *Undercurrents: A Life Beneath the Surface,* a memoir of her own experience with depression. Dr. Manning received her B.A. from the University of Maryland and her M.A. and Ph.D. in clinical psychology from The Catholic University of America. She completed a postdoctoral fellowship in clinical child psychology at McLean Hospital/Harvard Medical School. In addition to professional writing, she has written extensively in the popular press—with articles in *Health, Glamour, Mirabella, Ladies Home Journal, New Woman, The Washington Post,* and the *New York Times Book Review.* She has been featured in the Emmy-nominated HBO documentary "Dead Blue: Surviving Depression." Dr. Manning received the American Psychiatric Association's 1996 Presidential Award for Patient Advocacy and the 1999 Stephen V. Lang Award from NAMI for outstanding contribution by a psychologist to the understanding of brain disorders.

DREW PINSKY, M.D.

Drew Pinsky, M.D. is a specialist in internal medicine and a board-certified addictionologist. He is the medical director for the Department of Chemical Dependency Services at Las Encinas Hospital in Pasadena and the chief of service in the Department of Medicine. Dr. Pinsky is cohost of "Loveline," the nationally syndicated call-in radio and MTV program, which addresses relationships, love, and romance.

Last fall, Dr. Pinsky and his "Loveline" cohost Adam Carolla published *The Dr. Drew and Adam Book: A Survival Guide to Life and Love* (Dell Books), described as "the ultimate guide to life for the millennium." He is contributing editor to *USA Weekend* and Lawrence Neinstein's *Adolescent Health Care: A Parctical Guide.* Dr. Pinsky recently launched drdrew.com, the internet community for relationships, health, and lifestyle interests. He participates in weekly community discussions on addiction depression, and is a recipient of the Planned Parenthood and Shine Awards for his public education efforts.

Dr. Pinsky earned his medical degree from the University of Southern California (USC) School of Medicine, and his undergraduate degree from Amherst College in Amherst, Massachusetts. Dr. Pinsky completed his residency at USC and was later appointed Chief Resident. In addition, Dr. Pinsky served as the president of the Pasadena Medical Society and as the editor of the Los Angeles County Medical Association magazine.

LAURA EPSTEIN ROSEN, PH.D.

Laura Epstein Rosen, Ph.D., whose expertise is in depression and its impact on families and relationships, is a clinical psychologist and

109

Supervisor of Family Therapy Training, Department of Pediatric Psychiatry, at New York-Presbyterian Medical Center in New York. She also maintains a private practice for child, adult, and family psychotherapy and consults at the Adult AIDS Clinic at New York-Presbyterian. Dr. Rosen previously served as a family and couples therapist at the New York University Psychological Clinic, and worked in the family studies division at Beth Israel Medical Center.

Dr. Rosen contributes to numerous scientific publications on the subject of depression and its impact on families and relationships. She is also the coauthor of *When Someone You Love Is Depressed: How to Help Your Loved One without Losing Yourself.* She is frequently invited to speak at local support groups in the New York and New Jersey areas.

Dr. Rosen earned her graduate degree in clinical psychology from New York University and her undergraduate degree from Haverford College in Pennsylvania.

THOMAS N. WISE, M.D.

Thomas N. Wise, M.D. is a professor and Vice-Chair of the Department of Psychiatry at Georgetown University School of Medicine in Washington, DC, and Medical Director of Behavioral Services at Inova Health Systems in Falls Church, Virginia. In addition, he is Director of Research at the Sexual Behaviors Consultation Unit and professor of Psychiatry and Behavioral Sciences at Johns Hopkins School of Medicine in Baltimore, Maryland. Dr. Wise's major areas of professional interest include depression and sexual dysfunction in the medically ill, and personality factors in sexual disorders.

Dr. Wise earned his medical degree from Duke University School of Medicine and completed his undergraduate work at Dartmouth College. He completed residencies in psychiatry at Georgetown University Medical Center and the State University of New York Downstate Medical Center in Brooklyn, New York.

INDEX

Acute phase, 21
Aggressive behavior, 84
Agitation, 8, 83
Alcohol abuse, 9, 10, 25–26
Amador, Xavier Francisco, 87
American Academy of Child and
    Adolescent Psychiatry (AACAP), 93
American Association for Geriatric
    Psychiatry (AAGP), 93–94
American Association for Marriage and
    Family Therapy (AAMFT), 94
American Association of Suicidology
    (AAS), 100
American Foundation for Suicide
    Prevention (AFSP), 100
American Foundation for Urologic
    Disease (AFUD), 102
American Psychiatric Association
    (APA), 95
American Psychological Association
    (APA), 95
Anger, 83
Antidepressant medication, 8, 11,
    17–19; see also Medication chart
  addiction to, 28
  baseline level of functioning and,
    22, 24
  cost of, 24
  efficacy measures, 22–24
  insurance coverage and, 78–79
  nursing mothers and, 38
  as personality altering, 27
  physical symptoms, 23
  pregnancy and, 37
  sexual functioning, 24–25, 29, 51–54,
    66, 74–75, 88
  side effects of, 11, 22, 23, 26–27,
    28–29, 30–35

sources of information, 29
switching treatment, 22
therapy and, 19, 20
time for response to, 20, 23
treatment phases, 21
tricyclics and, 23, 27, 28–29, 30, 33,
    39, 74
weight gain and, 30
Anxiety, 8, 22, 83
Anxiety Disorders Association of
    America (ADAA), 94
Appetite changes; see Eating habit
    changes
Arousal, 33, 89
Auditory hallucinations, 6, 84

Bazelon Center, 95–96
Behavioral techniques, 20, 31
Bipolar disorder (manic depression), 6,
    11, 19, 53, 65, 73, 84
Blood disease, 11
Brain, chemistry of, 4
    medication and, 27, 28–29

Children, depression and, 67–69
Chronic depression, 5–6, 11
    defined, 5–6
    dysthymia, 6, 22
Clayton, Anita, 10, 20, 23, 24, 30, 32,
    33, 36, 37, 39, 41, 61, 107
Clergy, 8
Clinical depression, 5, 38, 84
    symptoms of, 5
    treatment of, 7–8, 18–19
Clinical social worker, 17
Cognitive behavioral therapy, 20
Cognitive impairment, 7
Communication, 62–63, 66

Concentration difficulties, 5, 6, 7, 11, 31, 83
Continuation phase, 21
Counselor, 17
Couples therapy, 47–48, 49– 50, 61, 63, 65
Crying, 83

Delusions, 6
Dementia, 11
Depression
    age of onset, 10
    atypical symptoms of, 29, 36
    children and home environment, 67–69
    education about, 4, 59
    in elderly, 10–11, 57–58
    finding a medical doctor, 73–77
    helping a partner, 45–46, 55–56, 58–60, 63–66
    managing symptoms of, 12
    as medical illness, 3–4
    in men versus women, 36–41
    occurrence of, 4
    other medical conditions and, 8–9
    personality and, 58
    phases of, 21
    predisposition to, 10
    recurrence of, 5, 9, 11
    self–diagnosis of, 7
    single episode, 5
    stigma of, 48–50
    symptoms of, 6–7, 54, 83–84
    treatment options, 7–8, 12, 18–19
    what is depression, 3–9
    who gets depression, 4, 10
Depression After Delivery, 96
Depression screening days, 7–8
Desire; see Sexual desire
Disconnection, 6
Drowsiness, 31–32
Drug abuse, 9, 10, 25–26, 28
Dunner, David, 4, 11, 21, 26, 29, 31, 34, 36, 48, 53, 65, 67, 74, 79, 107
Dysthymia, 6, 22

Eating habit changes, 5, 6, 7, 22, 30–31, 54, 83
ECT therapy;
    see Electroconvulsive therapy
Ejaculation, 33–34
Elderly, depression and, 10–11, 57
Electroconvulsive therapy (ECT), 34–35
Emotional intimacy, 55–65
    partners and depression, 66
Environmental factors, 4
Erectile dysfunction, 40, 54
Exhaustion, 5, 7, 8, 31, 83

Family counseling, 68
Family factors, 10, 69
Fatigue, 6, 7, 8, 10, 23, 50, 54
Friends, 7

Genetic factors, 4, 10, 69
Grieving, 5
Guilt, 6, 36, 38, 50, 83

Hearing voices, 6, 84
Hirschfeld, Robert, 6, 9, 11, 22, 27, 32, 45, 47, 66, 69, 74, 108
Hormone replacement therapy, 40

Inability to concentrate, 5, 6, 7, 10–11, 31, 83
Indecisiveness, 83
Indifference, 83
Information sources, mental health organizations, 93–100
Insomnia, 8; see also Sleep disturbances
Insurance coverage, 73, 77–79
Interpersonal therapy, 20
Intimacy, 33, 55, 64–65; see also Emotional intimacy
Irritability, 58, 83, 84

Lifestyle changes, 11
Lifetime maintenance treatment, 21
Loss of energy, 5, 31, 83
Loss of interest, 5, 6, 7

Loss of pleasure, 83
Loss of spouse, 11
Low energy, 8
Low mood, 7

Maintenance treatment, 21
Mania, symptom of, 83–84
Manic phase, 6
Manic-depression illness, 6, 11, 19, 53, 65, 73, 84
Manning, Martha, 3, 8, 12, 31, 35, 49, 56, 59, 60, 63, 68, 73, 76, 77, 108
MAO inhibitors, 29–30, 33
Medication; see Antidepressant medication
Medication chart, 104–105
Memory loss, 6–7
Men and depression, 36–41
   guided questionnaire for, 88–90
Menopause, 40
Men's Health Network (MHN), 101
Mental health coverage, 73, 77–79
Mental health organizations, 3, 93–99
Mental health professionals, 17, 84
Mild depression, 6, 20
Mood disorders, 38, 73, 84

National Alliance for the Mentally Ill (NAMI), 96
National Association of Social Workers (NASW), 97
National Depressive and Manic-Depressive Association (National DMDA), 4, 8, 17, 49, 50, 97
   support groups, 19, 65, 66, 78
National Foundation for Depressive Illness (NAFDI), 98
National Institute of Mental Health (NIMH), 98
National Mental Health Association (NMHA), 98–99
National Mental Illness Screening Project (NMISP), 99

National suicide hotline, 13
National Women's Health Resource Center (NWHRC), 101–102
NDRI, 29, 32, 52, 104
Night sweats, 32
Nutritionist, 30

Obsessive–Compulsive Foundation, 99
Open–door policy, therapy and, 63
Orgasm, 24–25, 29, 33–34, 90, 92
   antidepressant medication and, 39

Partners; see also Relationship problems
   depression and, 63–66
   helping a partner, 45–46, 58–60
   sexual dysfunction, 50–55
Personality, 58
Pessimism, 83
Physical complaints, 6
Physicians' Desk Reference (PDR), 29
Pinsky, Drew, 4, 9, 18, 22, 25, 28, 50, 52, 55, 56, 58, 62, 65, 74, 75, 109
Positive thinking, 7
Postpartum depression, 37–38
Pregnancy, 36–37
Primary care physician
   finding a doctor, 73–77
   as treatment referral source, 17, 58, 73
   visit checklist, 76
Psychiatrist, 9, 17, 58, 73, 78
Psychologist, 9, 17
Psychotherapist, 17
Psychotherapy, 17, 48, 52, 58, 66, 73
   treatment and medication, 18–19
Psychotic depression, 6
Psychotic features, 10

Questionnaire for men, 88–90
Questionnaire for women, 88, 91–92

Reckless behavior, 84
Recurrent depression, 11, 21

113

Relapse, 11, 21

Relationship problems, 5, 20, 33, 88–92;
   see also Sexual functioning
   communication and, 62–63, 66
   couples therapy, 47, 50, 61, 63, 65
   emotional intimacy and, 55–56
   helping a partner, 45–46, 58–60, 63–66
   questionnaire for, 85–87

Retirement, 11

Rosen, Laura Epstein, 18, 19, 26, 46, 47,
   48, 51, 52, 54, 57, 58, 61, 64,
   78, 87, 109

Sadness, 6, 7, 83

St. John's wort, 35–36

Seasonal depression, 11

Segraves, Kathleen, 92

Segraves, R. Taylor, 92

Selective serotonin reuptake inhibitors
   (SSRIs), 23, 29, 30, 32, 33, 34, 39,
   52, 74

Self tests, 83–87

Senility, 11

Serotonin, 32, 34

Sexual desire (sex drive), 5, 6, 7, 23, 34,
   40, 50, 88–92

Sexual Function Health Council, 102

Sexual functioning, 33–34, 47, 56
   helping your partner, 50–55
   medication and, 24–25, 32–34,
     74–75, 88
   performance phases, 33

Shame, 19, 49

Short-term therapies, 20

Sleep disturbances, 5, 7, 20–21, 22, 23,
   31–32, 54, 83

Social withdrawal, 64, 83

Social worker, 17, 78

SSRI; see Selective serotonin reuptake
   inhibitors

SSRIB, 29, 32, 52, 105

Stigma of depression, 48–50

Stimulants, 8

Stress, 5, 7, 88

Suicidal thoughts, 5, 6, 7, 22, 74, 83
   alcohol abuse and, 25
   seeking help, 12–13, 46

Suicide, 6, 10, 12

Suicide Prevention Advocacy Network
   (SPAN), 101

Suicide Prevention Organizations,
   100–101

Support groups, 17, 19, 60, 78

Sweating, 32

Talk therapy, 19, 48; see also
   Psychotherapy
   affording treatment, 78
   finding mental health professionals, 17
   therapist–patient relationship, 17–18

Tetracyclics, 29, 30, 32, 52, 105

Therapy, sharing with loved ones, 3, 26,
   47–48, 63

Thyroid disturbance, 11

Tiredness, 5, 31, 83

Treatment options, 7–8, 12, 18–19

Tricyclics, 23, 27, 28, 29, 30, 33, 39, 74

Unipolar disorder, 11

Web sites, 8

Weight gain, 30–31

Wise, Thomas, 5, 7, 21, 24, 38, 39, 40,
   52, 53, 54, 110

Women and depression, 10, 36–41
   antidepressants and weight gain,
     30–31
   guided questionnaire for, 88, 91–92
   interpersonal therapy and, 20
   menopause and, 40–41
   nursing mothers, 37–38
   postpartum depression, 37–38
   pregnancy and, 36–37

Worry, 83

Worthlessness, 6, 54, 57, 83

BECOME AN ANNUAL MEMBER!

Support the efforts of National DMDA to improve availability and quality of health care, eliminate discrimination and stigma, develop strong local affiliates, enhance partnerships with the professional health care community, and support research.

New members will automatically receive a copy of *A Guide to Depressive and Manic-Depressive Illness: Diagnosis, Treatment, and Support,* a National DMDA *Bookstore Catalog,* a National DMDA *Chapter Directory,* and a subscription to the *Outreach* newsletter (published four times a year.)

APPLICATION

Name _____

Address _____

_____

City _____

State _____ Zip _____

Daytime Telephone _____

☐ Individual $20   ☐ Household $35

☐ Professional $100   ☐ Lifetime $750

☐ Individual memberships are $15 for dues-paying members of DMDA chapters or support groups. To qualify, you must include a letter from a chapter leader stating you are current in local dues or proof of paid membership.

DMDA Chapter Affiliation _____

(Membership payments in U.S. dollars. Add $10 if outside U.S.A.)

I would also like to make a donation to National DMDA: $_____

TOTAL PAYMENT ENCLOSED: $_____

Method of Payment

☐ Check *(payable to National DMDA)*

☐ Money order

☐ VISA

☐ MasterCard

Account No. _____ Exp. Date _____

Signature _____

Mail payment to: National DMDA
730 N. Franklin St., Suite 501
Chicago, IL 60610-3526 USA

Questions? Call (800) 826-3632 or (312) 642-0049

Credit card applications (Visa or MasterCard) may be faxed to (312) 642-7243

National DMDA is a not-for-profit organization. Your contributions may be tax deductible. For more information, please consult your tax advisor.

Thank you!